KU-677-398

Praise for David McCandless

'Unbelievably brilliant' Vogue

'(A) terrific compendium of visual information' Shortlist

'In this intriguing book, David McCandless presents a cavalcade of compelling and colourful graphics, each one innovative in its attempt to offer a new perspective on some of our most pervasive twenty-first century obsessions' Time Out

'Stunning' The Sunday Times

'Thought-provoking, lovingly-crafted and informative; a handsome book that anyone would be grateful to receive' Independent on Sunday

'What David McCandless has done is genius... dry data is transformed into small pieces of pop art that engage so much you end up learning more, without realising it. The ideal encyclopaedia for the information age' Red Handed

beautiful news

beautiful news

David McCandless

WILLIAM
COLLINS

William Collins
An imprint of HarperCollinsPublishers
1 London Bridge Street
London SE1 9GF

WilliamCollinsBooks.com

HarperCollinsPublishers
1st Floor, Watermarque Building, Ringsend Road
Dublin 4, Ireland

First published in Great Britain by William Collins in 2021

2024 2023 2022 2021
2 4 6 8 10 9 7 5 3 1

First published in the United States by HarperDesign, an imprint of HarperCollinsPublishers in 2021

Copyright © David McCandless 2021

www.davidmccandless.com

David McCandless asserts the moral right to be identified as the author of this work in accordance with the Copyright, Designs and Patents Act 1988

A catalogue record for this book is available from the British Library

ISBN 978-0-00-744837-1

All rights reserved. No part of this publication may be reproduced, stored in a retrieval system, or transmitted, in any form or by any means, electronic, mechanical, photocopying, recording or otherwise, without the prior permission of the publishers.

This book is sold subject to the condition that it shall not, by way of trade or otherwise, be lent, re-sold, hired out or otherwise circulated without the publisher's prior consent in any form of binding or cover other than that in which it is published and without a similar condition including this condition being imposed on the subsequent purchaser.

Printed and bound in Bosnia and Herzegovina by GPS Group

MIX
Paper from
responsible sources
FSC
www.fsc.org   FSC™ C007454

dedicated to all those uncelebrated millions
who work quietly and steadily
to make the world a better place

Introduction

This is Beautiful News. Some of the amazing, beautiful, positive things happening in the world that we can't see because we're fixated on the negativity of the news.

If the news is your main window on the world – as it is for me – it's difficult not to see it as an infernal hellscape of conflict, murder, disagreement, tragedy and violence.

At best that's an unfair depiction of the world. At worse it's false, distorting and mentally harmful.

A function of charts and graphics has always been to show us what we can't naturally see. In this case, the slow developments, quiet trends that go unseen, uncelebrated. Decadal increases. Generational shifts. Historic reductions. Incremental change. Subtle upticks. The slow and steady symphony of progress.

Without these views, it's easy to succumb to doom, pessimism, powerlessness. The scale and complexity of the world's problems feels overwhelming. But often *understanding* can be the antidote.

That's why this book is not just beautiful trends, but also full of infographic primers – visual explainers of complex but important topics – so you can better understand them as they pop up in the news.

Working closely with these topics and all the surrounding data and information over the months, I've noticed a shift in myself and my outlook. I feel less heavy. A bit brighter. Maybe even ...a little hopeful?

The world is not perfect. It never will be. But nor is it as bad as it looks. That's clear.

I get this feeling that optimism is a muscle. One that can be supported by regular exercise and a diet of healthy information. So if the news is fast food – tasty and moreish but unhealthy – then take this book as a beautiful salad. Full of fresh ideas and nutritious perspectives to revitalise your mind, strengthen your heart and give you something delicious to chew on...

David McCandless, June 2021

Fewer Children Are Dying

% dying before the age of five worldwide

43%

1820

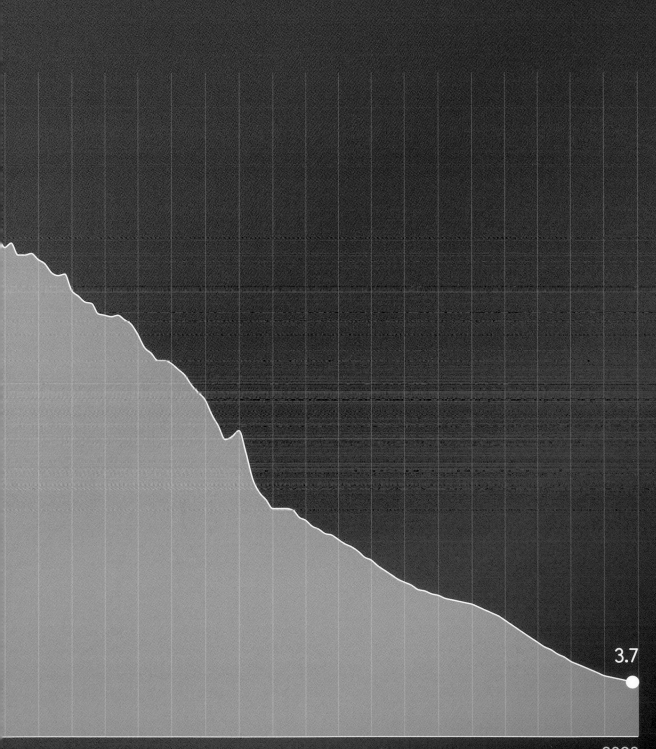

3.7

2020

source: Our World in Data

Foreign Aid Has Exploded
Money given to poorer nations

SOCIAL
ECONOMIC
PRODUCTION
MULTISECTOR

 $4bn

DEBT RELIEF
COMMODITY
HUMANITARIAN
UNSPECIFIED

1960

$163

2000   2017

source: OECD, constant dollars

Women Can Finally Vote Everywhere*

% of countries

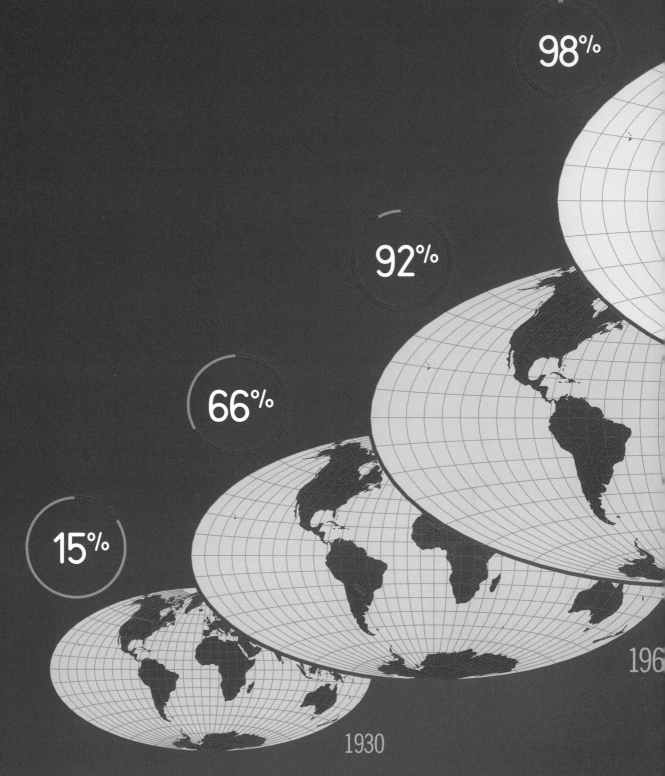

98%

92%

66%

15%

1930

196

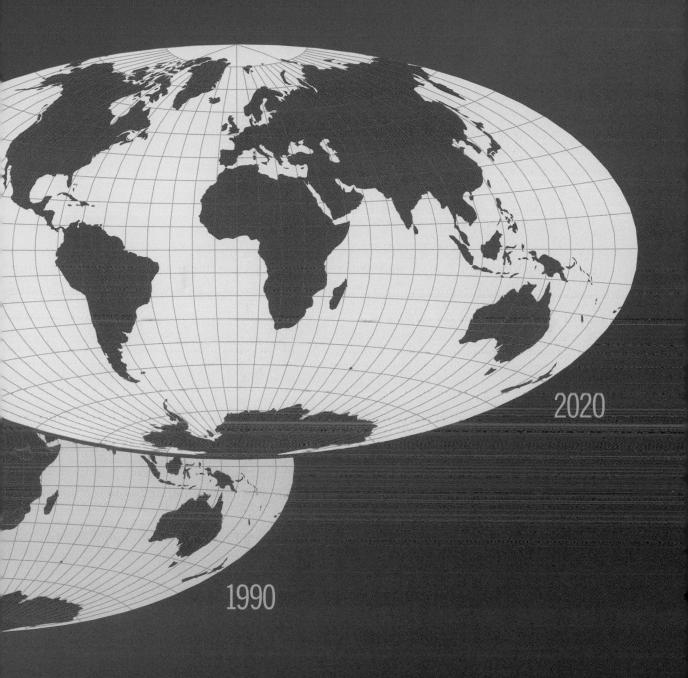

2020

1990

*except Vatican City and Brunei

source: Pew Research Center

World Hunger Has Reached Its Lowest Point in 20 Years

Angola

Sierra Leone

13%

2000

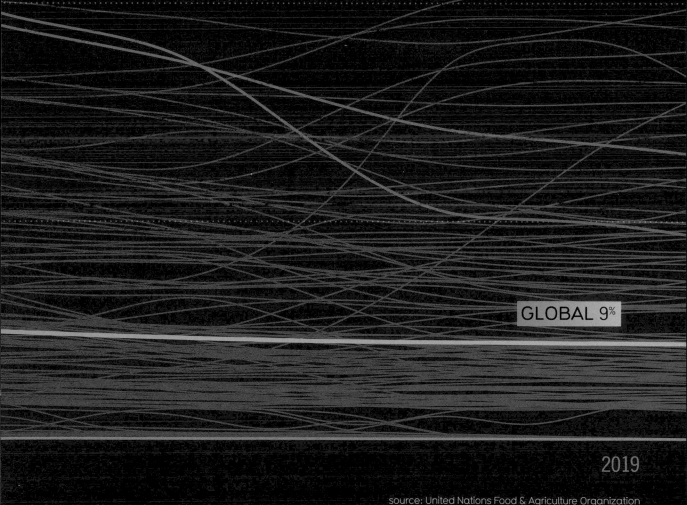

GLOBAL 9%

2019

source: United Nations Food & Agriculture Organization

We've Decommissioned 85% of the World's Nukes

Thousands of nuclear warheads

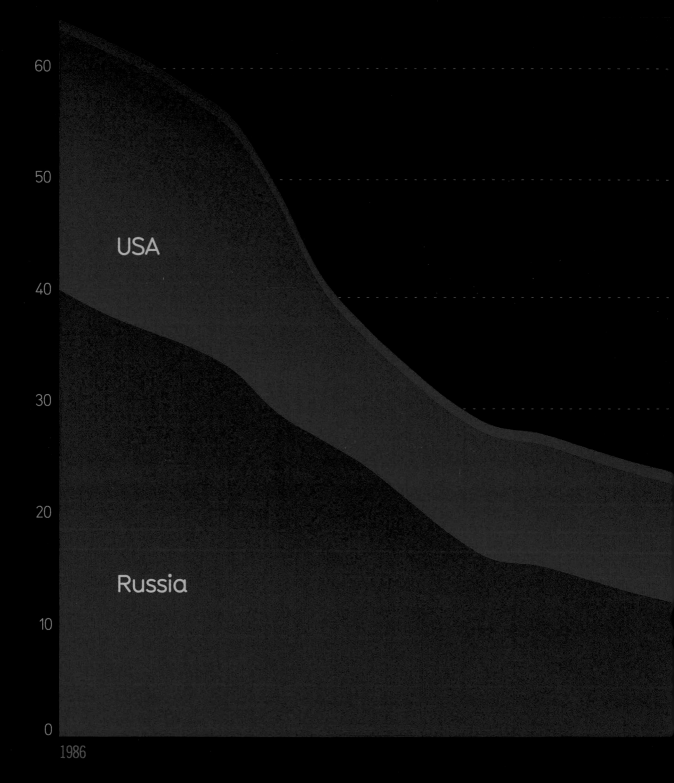

USA

Russia

1986

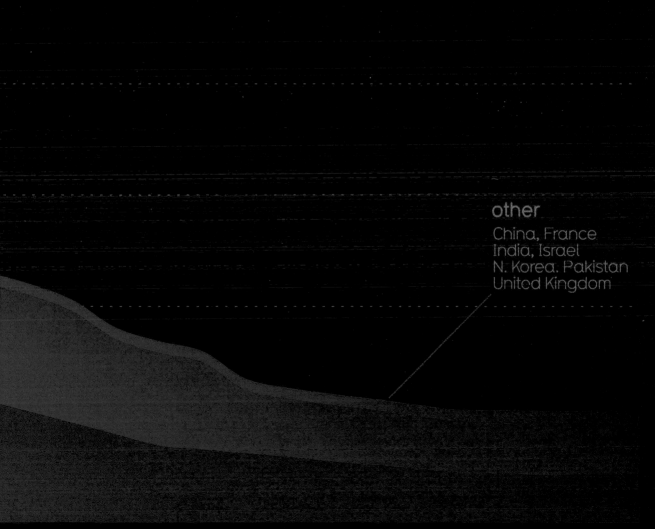

other
China, France
India, Israel
N. Korea. Pakistan
United Kingdom

2017

Humpback Whales Are Recovering

125,000
whales worldwide

1500

135,000
9 of 14 humpback populations
are no longer endangered

10,000
whaling ban imposed

1966

2019

sources: US National Park Service, Endangered Species Coalition

The world will solar panels **EVERY HOUR** over the next three years

add 70,000

source: Our World in Data

Extreme Poverty Is Decreasing
% world population living on less than $1.90 per day

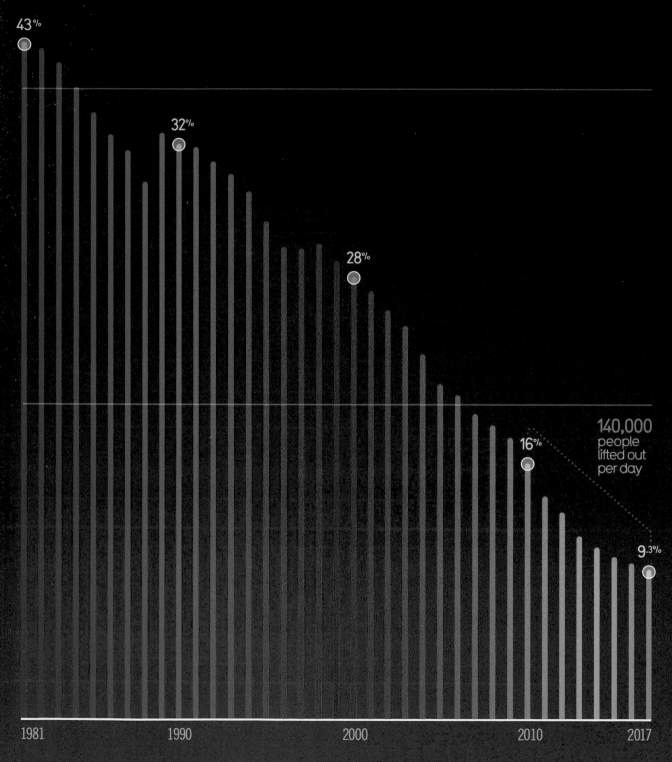

43%

32%

28%

16%

9.3%

140,000
people
lifted out
per day

1981   1990   2000   2010   2017

source: Our World in Data

More Than Half the World Now
Lives in a Democracy

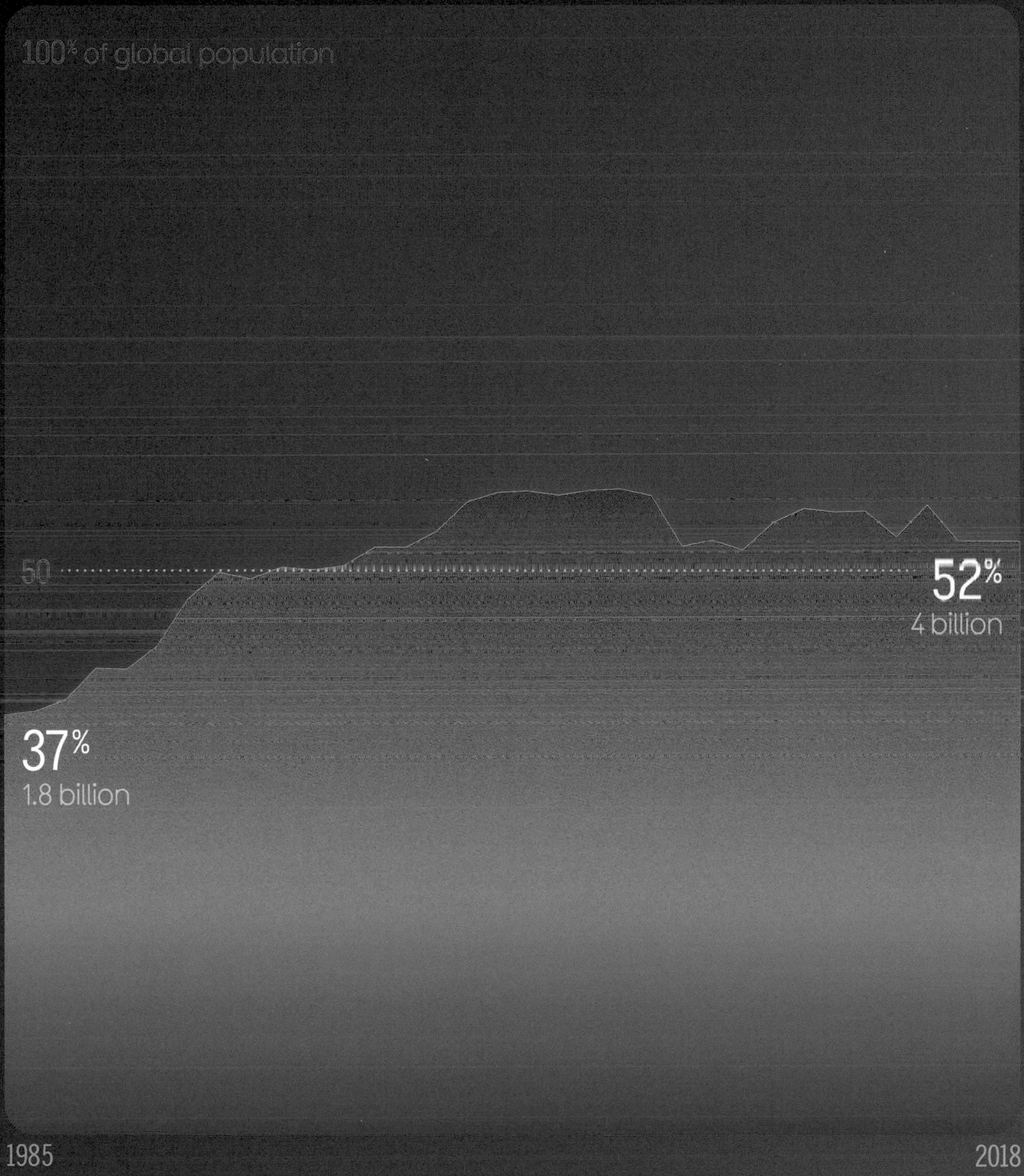

100% of global population

50

52%
4 billion

37%
1.8 billion

1985

2018

source: Our World in Data

Billions More Can Now Drink Safely

world population with access to safe water

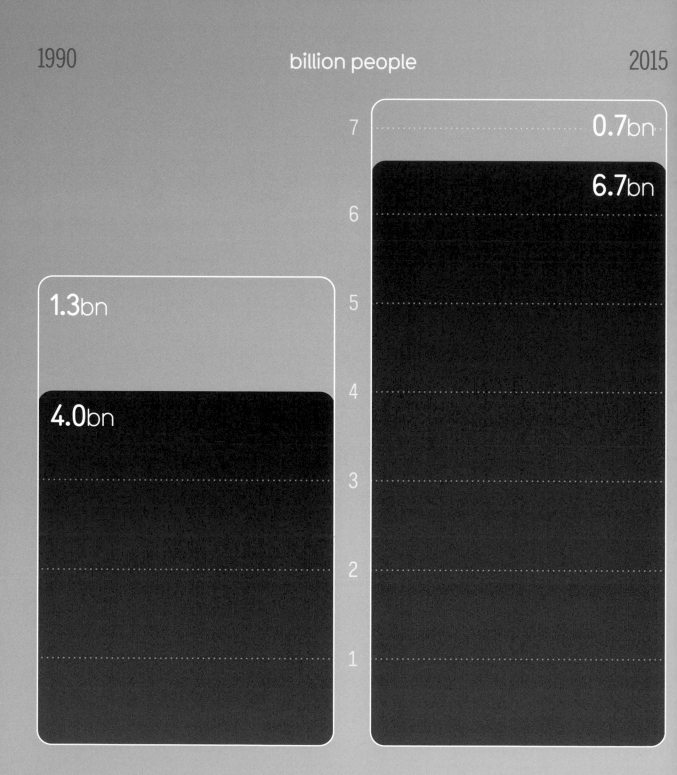

1990

billion people

2015

0.7bn

6.7bn

1.3bn

4.0bn

7

6

5

4

3

2

1

sources: Our World in Data, World Water

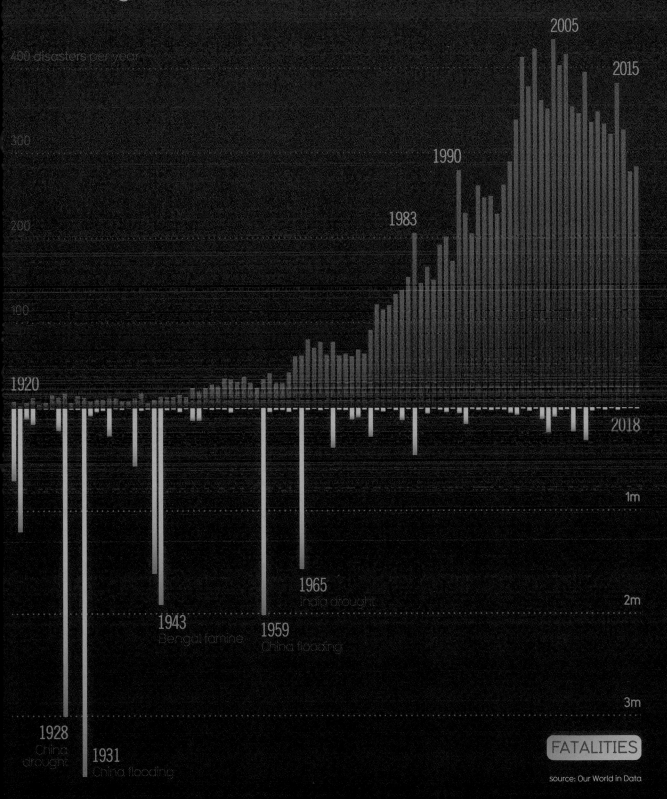

Natural Disasters Are Far Less Deadly
Floods, droughts, hurricanes & earthquakes

400 disasters per year

300

200

100

1920

2005

2015

1990

1983

2018

1m

1965
India drought

2m

1943
Bengal famine

1959
China flooding

3m

1928
China
drought

1931
China flooding

FATALITIES

source: Our World in Data

Fewer Women Are Dying of Breast Cancer
Deaths per 100,000

31.4
1975

19.7
2018

sources: Queen Mary University London, National Cancer Institute

Cancer Survival Rates Are Rising

% alive five years after diagnosis

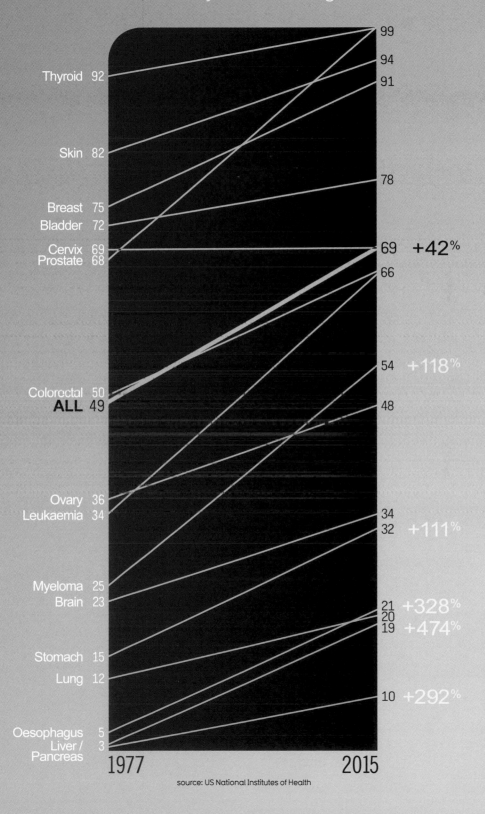

	1977	2015
		99
		94
Thyroid	92	91
Skin	82	
		78
Breast	75	
Bladder	72	
Cervix	69	69 +42%
Prostate	68	66
		54 +118%
Colorectal	50	48
ALL	49	
Ovary	36	34
Leukaemia	34	32 +111%
Myeloma	25	
Brain	23	21 +328%
		20
		19 +474%
Stomach	15	
Lung	12	
		10 +292%
Oesophagus	5	
Liver / Pancreas	3	

source: US National Institutes of Health

The Best Things in Life Really Are Free
What makes people most happy, according to data?

leisure
6%

bonding
10%

nature
3%

achievement
34%

affection
34%

enjoying
the moment
11%

exercise
2%

sources: Flowing Data, Happy DB

Far More Unites Us Than Divides Us
% average similarity in common values between groups

between
countries
84%

between
religions
91%

between
rich & poor
96%

between
genders
97%

between
age groups
96%

between
education levels
96%

Britain's Woodland Cover Is Returning to Medieval Levels
total land area coverage

15%
1086

2020

5%
1919

thanks to 20th-century forestry and the 'rewilding' trend

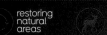

restoring
natural
areas

re-introducing
wild animal
species

planting
native
trees

Simple Oral Rehydration Therapy Has Saved Millions of Lives Around the World

Treating diarrhoea is **easy, cheap** (0.20$/day) & **accessible**

GLUCOSE	31%
SODIUM	31%
CHLORIDE	27%
POTASSIUM	8%
CITRATE	4%

given to
millions
of kids under five
worldwide every year

And thanks to an improved formula with zinc, deaths are still falling around the world

2.4 million
under-five
deaths from
diarrhoea
worldwide

880,000

2000   2017

source: WHO, USAID

Over Two Billion More People Have Gained Access to Improved Sanitation

5bn

2.8bn

53%
of world population

68%

1990   2015

source: Our World in Data

The EU has banned bee-harming pesticides

source: European Food Safety Authority

Pakistan has met its climate goals one decade before the United Nations deadline

planted billions
of trees in
just two years!

ranked &
rewarded its
cleanest cities

protected up to
15% of its parks
& wildlife areas

source: Good News Network

Land Devoted to Producing Meat & Milk Is Beginning to Shrink Again

30%

23.9%

24.8%

20%

1961   2018

source: United Nations Food & Agriculture Organization

Healthy Life Expectancy Is Increasing in Almost Every Country

2000–2018

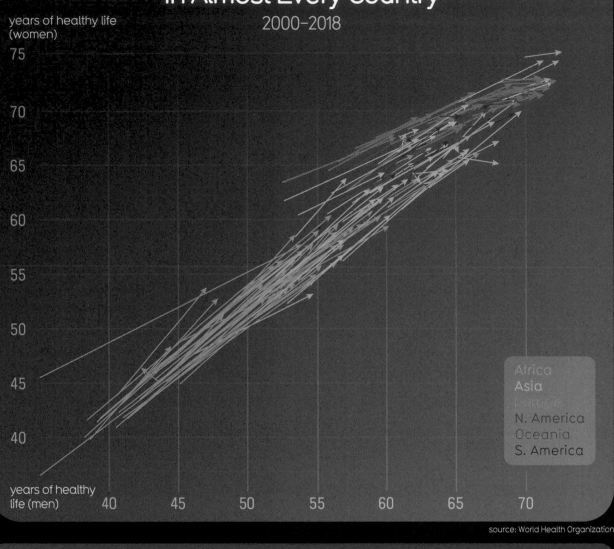

years of healthy life (women)

75

70

65

60

55

50

45

40

years of healthy life (men)

40   45   50   55   60   65   70

Africa
Asia
Europe
N. America
Oceania
S. America

source: World Health Organization

Homicides Are Falling Around the World % decrease 1998–2018

World Average −15%

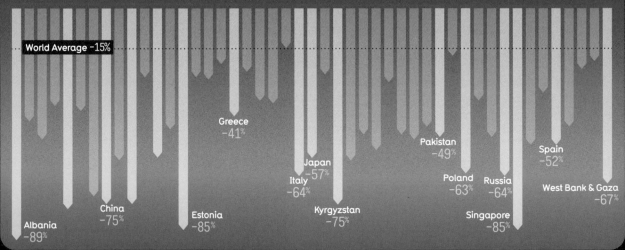

Albania −89%

China −75%

Estonia −85%

Greece −41%

Italy −64%
Japan −57%

Kyrgyzstan −75%

Pakistan −49%

Poland −63%

Singapore −85%

Russia −64%

Spain −52%

West Bank & Gaza −67%

source: World Bank

The HPV Vaccine Has Slashed Infections
% prevalence among sexually active females aged 14-24

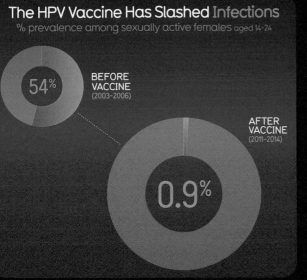

54% BEFORE VACCINE (2003–2006)

AFTER VACCINE (2011–2014)

0.9%

source: Journal of Infectious Diseases, USA data

The US Gender Pay Gap Is Shrinking (Slowly)
% difference between male & female pay

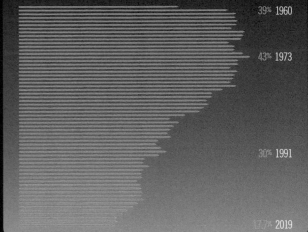

39% 1960

43% 1973

30% 1991

17.7% 2019

source: US Census Bureau, average pay

Road Travel in the US Is Safer than Ever
Fatalities per 100m vehicle miles travelled

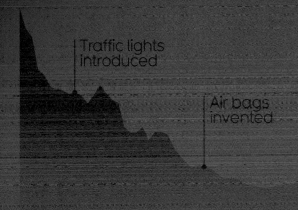

650,000 lives saved

Traffic lights introduced

Air bags invented

Five-star safety ratings introduced

24 deaths

1.1

Country-wide safety standards established

First seatbelts in US cars

1921   1930   1950   1968   1993   2019

source: National Highway Traffic Safety Administration

Eleven Diseases We've Nearly Controlled or Eradicated

on our way

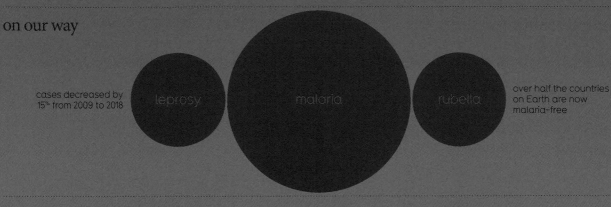

cases decreased by 15% from 2009 to 2018

leprosy

malaria

rubella

over half the countries on Earth are now malaria-free

progress!

AKA 'elephantiasis' a lesser-known tropical disease spread by mosquitoes

onchocerciasis

rabies

yaws

India was the first country to eradicate this terrible disease of childhood in 2016

lymphatic filariasis

Chronic parasitic disease caused by microscopic, thread-like worms spread by mosquito bites

nearly...

'sleeping sickness' spread by tsetse flies

African trypano-somiasis

polio

guinea-worm disease

terrible affliction spread by contaminated drinking water

eradicated

smallpox

size = global impact of disease

sources: World Health Organisation, Our World in Data

Quick Quiz

What % of people in the world.... PTO for answers

...live in extreme poverty?

...can now read and write?

...live in high- or middle-income nations?

...have some access to electricity?

Overall, compared to 25 years ago, do you think the world today is

worse?
the same?
better?
substantially better?

Quick Quiz:
Answers

How close were you?

9%

86%

91%

89%

beautiful news

source: Our World in Data

These People Donate $1 Billion Every...

 61 DAYS
MacKenzie Scott
EX-WIFE OF JEFF BEZOS

 126
Warren Buffet
FAMOUS INVESTOR

 184
Bill & Melinda Gates

 227
Chan & Mark Zuckerberg

 586
George Soros

 606
Michael Bloomberg

 7.5 YEARS
Jeff Bezos

 20 YEARS
Elon Musk

% of Net Worth Given Away

16%
Warren Buffet

10%
MacKenzie Scott

9%
Bill & Melinda Gates

5%
Michael Bloomberg

0.1
(before 2020)
5%
Jeff Bezos
(after 2020)

2%
Chan & Mark Zuckerberg

37%
George Soros

 0.06%
Elon Musk

sources: World Economic Forum, EcoWatch, New York Times

Finland Is Teaching Kids to Identify Fake News

Professional methods are taught across all subjects

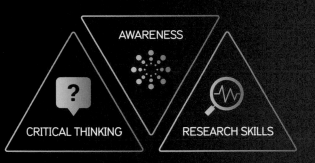

AWARENESS

CRITICAL THINKING

RESEARCH SKILLS

Finland Has Europe's highest media literacy

Index on how resilient a country's population is to fake news

Country	Index
Finland	76
Denmark	
Netherlands	70
Sweden	
Estonia	
Ireland	
Belgium	
Germany	
Iceland	
UK	60
Slovenia	
Austria	
Spain	
Luxembourg	
Portugal	
France	
Latvia	
Poland	
Czech Rep.	
Lithuania	
Italy	50
Slovakia	
Malta	
Croatia	
Cyprus	
Hungary	40
Greece	
Romania	
Serbia	
Bulgaria	30
Montenegro	
Bosnia	
Albania	
Turkey	
N. Macedonia	10

source: Open Society Institute (Bulgaria)

We Are Starting to Ban Fossil-Fuel Vehicles

● all cars ○ new cars

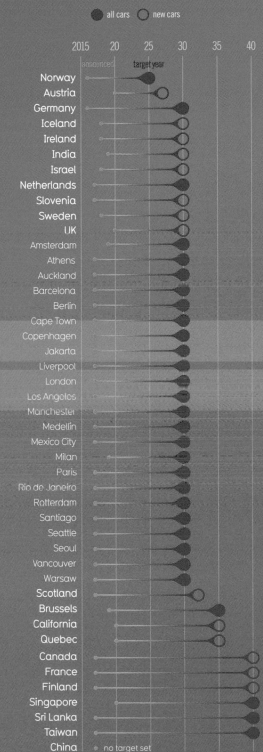

2015 (announced) · target year · 20 · 25 · 30 · 35 · 40

Norway, Austria, Germany, Iceland, Ireland, India, Israel, Netherlands, Slovenia, Sweden, UK, Amsterdam, Athens, Auckland, Barcelona, Berlin, Cape Town, Copenhagen, Jakarta, Liverpool, London, Los Angeles, Manchester, Medellín, Mexico City, Milan, Paris, Rio de Janeiro, Rotterdam, Santiago, Seattle, Seoul, Vancouver, Warsaw, Scotland, Brussels, California, Quebec, Canada, France, Finland, Singapore, Sri Lanka, Taiwan, China

China — no target set

sources: Guardian, BBC, Independent and others

Millions of Childrens' Lives Have Been Saved

725
per day

265,000
per year

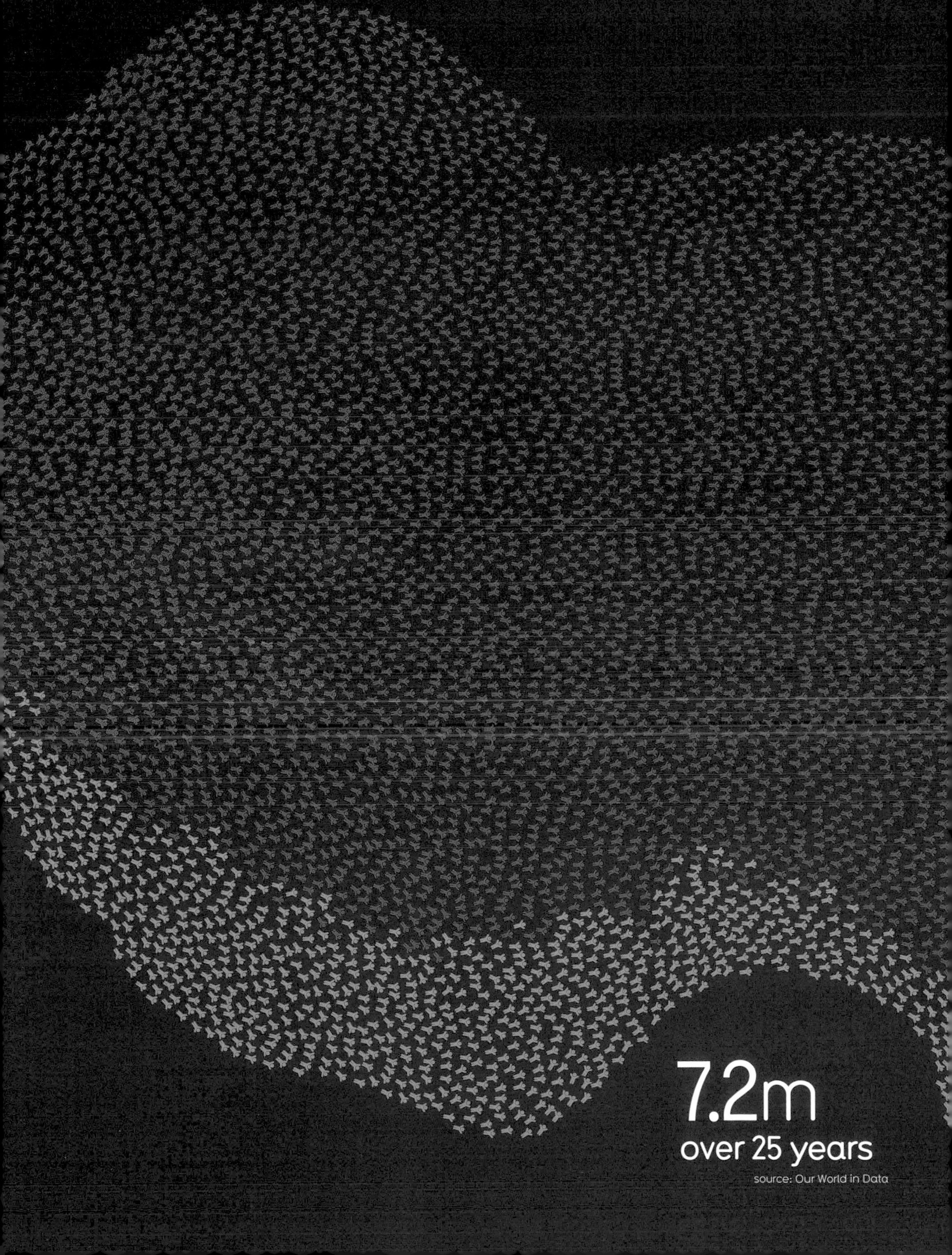

7.2m
over 25 years
source: Our World in Data

Millions of Childrens' Lives Are Being Saved

Preterm Infant Deaths Are Down
Deaths per 100,000 babies

200

160

-52%

120

80

40

1990   2017

source: Our World in Data

Newborn Deaths Have Halved
Deaths per 1,000 live births

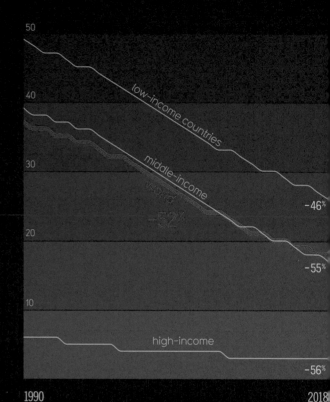

50

40   low-income countries

30   middle-income

                world   -52%   -46%

20   -55%

10

          high-income
                                             -56%

1990   2018

source: World Bank

Every Disease that Kills Children Is Declining
% reduction in the last decade

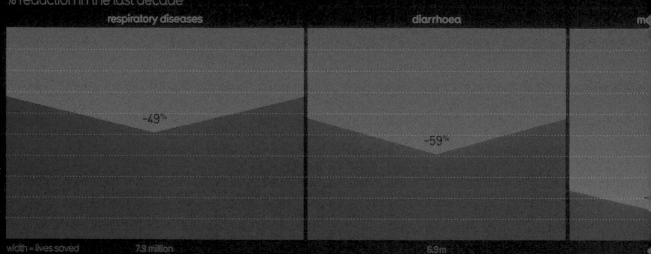

respiratory diseases   diarrhoea   me

-49%   -59%

width = lives saved   7.9 million   6.9m

Infant Deaths Have More than Halved
Deaths per 1,000 births wordwide

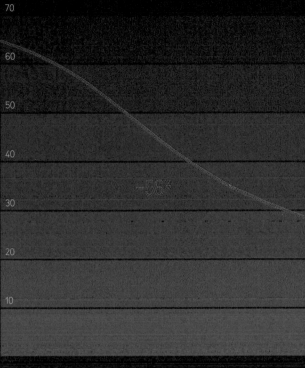

70
60
50
40
30
-56%
20
10

1990   2019

source: World Bank

Kids Deaths Declined Worldwide
% of children dying before five years old

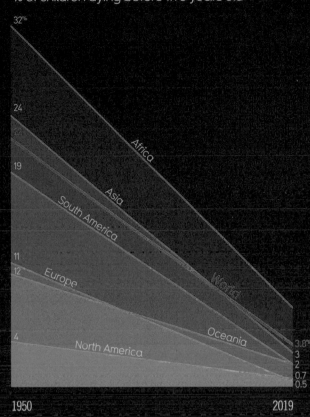

32%

24
22
19

Africa

Asia

South America

11
12   Europe

4   World

                    North America   Oceania

3.8%
3
2
0.7
0.5

1950   2019

source: Our World in Data

26 million lives saved

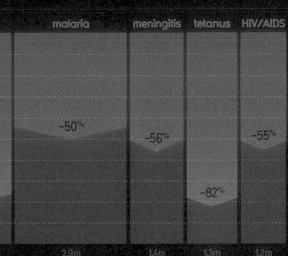

malaria	meningitis	tetanus	HIV/AIDS
-50%	-56%		-55%
		-82%	
2.9m	1.4m	1.3m	1.2m

source: World Health Organization

What Children Die From
Thousand deaths per year

newborn disorders
1,784
premature birth, sepsis etc

infectious diseases
991
malaria, HIV/AIDS, meningitis, measles

respiratory infections
870
pneumonia, tuberculosis

intestinal infections
578
diarrhoea mostly

injuries & accidents
270

non-communicable diseases
170

other
584

source: Our World in Data

better education of women

increasing spending

higher-quality healthcare

improving health knowledge

Child Deaths & the Education of Mothers are Inter-Related

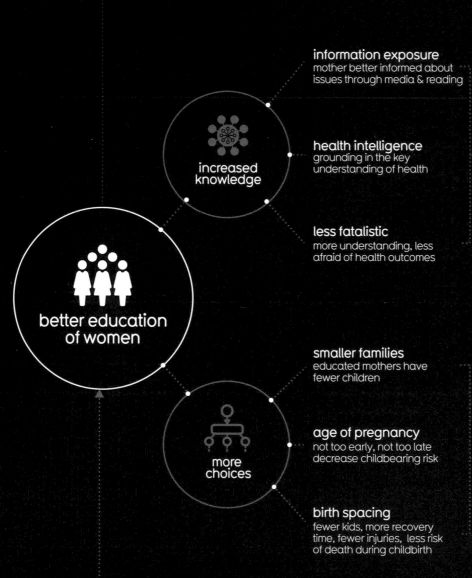

information exposure
mother better informed about
issues through media & reading

better interactions
medical staff more likely
to listen to educated mothers

increased knowledge

health intelligence
grounding in the key
understanding of health

more empowerment

mor
contr

less fatalistic
more understanding, less
afraid of health outcomes

more confident
handling bureacracy,
decisions, choices, etc.

can also ignore
outdated advice
from family members

better education of women

smaller families
educated mothers have
fewer children

more choices

age of pregnancy
not too early, not too late
decrease childbearing risk

birth spacing
fewer kids, more recovery
time, fewer injuries, less risk
of death during childbirth

may choose to become a
health professional and
help other mothers

increasing
education

rising
prosperity

declining
poverty

Educated mothers more
likely to receive:
• prenatal care
• immunisations
• trained personnel at
  their deliveries

a

proper feeding
educated mothers have
fewer children

**better birth
outcomes**

**MOTHER
SURVIVES**

**baby's health
thrives**

immunisation
not too early, not too late
decrease childbearing risk

diarrhoea medicine
Educated mothers use
oral rehydration salts

incredibly affordable &
simple intervention that
saves children's lives

diarrhoea kills

10 %of kids
under five

but since 2000
deaths have declined

source: E. Gakidou et al., Lancet 2010

More Girls Are in School

Female & Male Literacy Rates Have Almost Equalised Worldwide

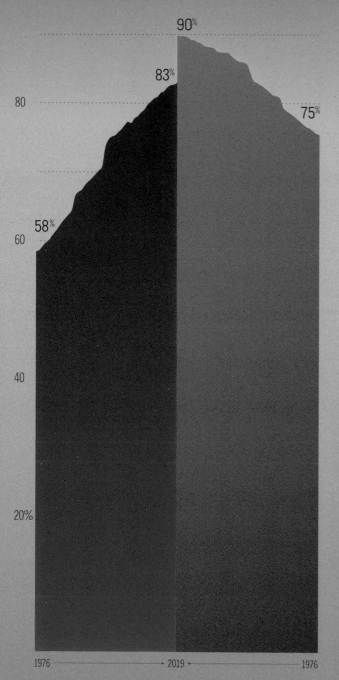

100

90%

83%

80

75%

58%

60

40

20%

1976 — 2019 — 1976

Girls Not in Primary School Have Fallen to an All-Time Low

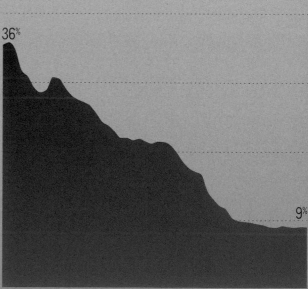

36%

9%

1970   2019

Even More Girls Are Enrolling in Secondary School

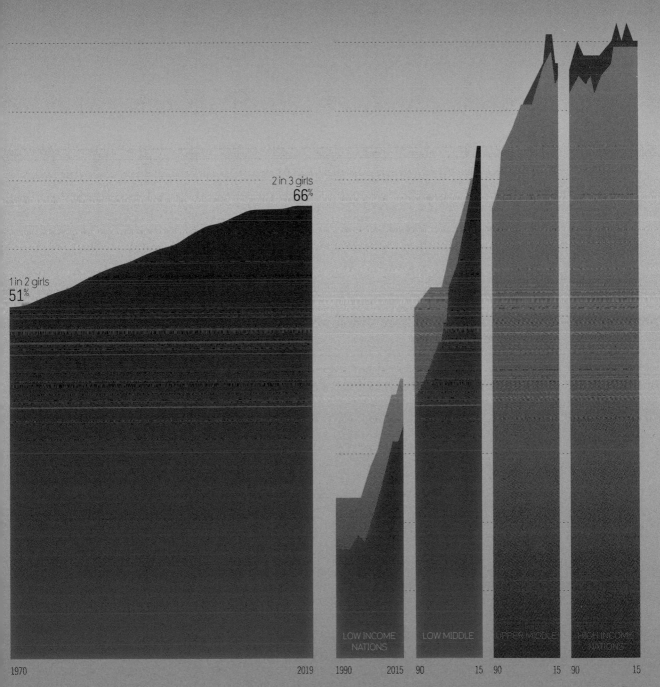

2 in 3 girls
66%

1 in 2 girls
51%

1970   2019

The Education Gender Gap between Girls & Boys Is Closing

% completing school

LOW INCOME
NATIONS

LOW MIDDLE

UPPER MIDDLE

HIGH INCOME
NATIONS

1990   2015   90   15   90   15   90   15

source: World Bank

Things Going Up! Up! Up!
improving substantially, globally

Life Expectancy
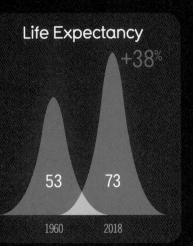
+38%
53 — 1960
73 — 2018

Domestic Violence Laws
% countries covered

0% — 1970
85% — 2019

Leaf Area
% increase per decade

+5%   +10%

Mexico
USA
Australia
Russia
Canada
EU
India
China

Global Health Spending
$ per person

+154%
$846
$323
2005   2018

Meat Substitutes
yearly revenue $bn
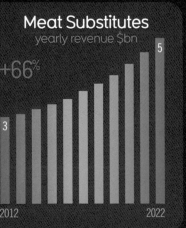
+66%
3
5
2012   2022

Same-Sex Union
countries where legal
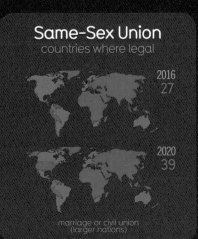
2016
27
2020
39
marriage or civil union
(larger nations)

Global Literacy

1976   2020
69%   86%
+25%

The Happiest Countries in the World?

Senegal Mozambique Ethiopia
Nigeria Uruguay N.Macedonia Czech Republic
Chad **United Arab Emirates** Zambia
Myanmar **New Zealand** Indonesia
Panama Brazil Tajikistan Algeria
Uzbekistan Vietnam Kuwait Taiwan Malta
Portugal Bosnia & Herzegovina **Canada** Lebanon Mauritius
Dominican Republic **Denmark** Iraq Liberia Serbia
Niger Mauritania El Salvador
Spain **Germany** Mongolia Kenya Japan **Ireland** Georgia
Saudi Arabia Albania **Iceland** **Costa Rica**
Botswana Chile **Israel** Slovenia Cyprus
Libya China DR Congo South Korea
Iran Kosovo Jamaica Uganda Peru Bangladesh Namibia Laos Guatemala Cambodia
Madagascar **Switzerland** Colombia
Montenegro Italy Romania Jordan Benin **Belgium** Ukraine
India South Sudan **Netherlands** Russia Morocco
Gabon Sri Lanka Slovakia Yemen Pakistan
France Croatia United States Guinea **Austria** Hungary
Azerbaijan **Norway** Kyrgyzstan Latvia Greece
Mexico Haiti
Belarus **Sweden** Sierra Leone Togo Tunisia
Moldova Egypt Argentina Nepal Palestine Cameroon Turkey
Nicaragua **Finland** Armenia Lithuania
Estonia Mali
Luxembourg Central African Republic Ghana
Philippines Afghanistan Zimbabwe Honduras
Turkmenistan **Australia** Trinidad & Tobago
Bulgaria Malawi **United Kingdom** South Africa
Singapore Ecuador Bahrain Burkina Faso Thailand Kazakhstan
Hong Kong Congo Ivory Coast
Poland Tanzania Bolivia

source: The World Happiness Report 2020

But these ratings use a Western definition of 'happiness'

Which centres more on 'vertical' feelings
of individualism & 'independence'

known as **happiness**

FACTORS

freedom
autonomy to do what
I want, when I want,
how I want

thrilling experiences
pleasure-seeking,
novelty, intensity,
variety

positive emotions
intense high-arousal
feelings like excitement,
cheerfulness

achievement
success, recognition,
material gains, often linked
to hard work

individualism
my journey
my story
my life

positivity
preferably full or
overflowing with
no negative feelings

development
growth, self-improvement
in a linear fashion with an
individualised 'purpose'

self-esteem
an ongoing internal
feeling of
personal value

Different cultures have differing definitions of 'happiness'

For instance, Eastern happiness is more 'horizontal',
focusing on relationships & connections

known as interdependent **happiness**

FACTORS

social harmony
sychronising with others,
not causing problems
or stress for others

relationships
meaning & purpose
through nurtured
social connections

low arousal
stability, absence
of major anxieties
or concerns

interpersonal goals
improving relationships,
focus on making
others happy

collectivism
feeling of being part
of a much larger
whole

ordinariness
similarity with others,
just catching up
with others

equity
equality of
accomplishment
with one's peers

'obedience'
being able to meet
other's expectations
of oneself

source: Hitokoto 2014,JICA Ogata Sadako Research Institute for Peace & Development

The Happiest Countries in the World

in terms of 'interdependent happiness'

countries highly ranked on both scales

Lithuania France
Germany Switzerland
Slovakia Netherlands Pakistan
Sweden Estonia Malaysia Palestine
Vietnam Chile Nigeria Portugal Bulgaria
Greece Turkey Serbia Thailand
Canada Romania USA South Africa
Jordan Italy Bolivia China Peru UK Japan
Uganda Slovenia Norway Czechia
Poland Israel Croatia Colombia
Ukraine Taiwan Mexico Senegal Kenya
Hungary Brazil Russia Philippines
Latvia Denmark S.Korea Georgia
Spain Indonesia
Austria Hong Kong
Argentina Belgium Singapore
New Zealand Australia
N.Macedonia

note: not all nations have been rated for interdependent happiness, so may be missing

source: Cross-Cultural Happiness, Gardiner et al, 2020

Global Flavours of Happiness & Contentment

putuwa

Warming one's hands by the fire while gently squeezing someone else's hands

GADIGAL
(aboriginal)

عشرة

eshra

Connectedness and obligations arising from people having known each other a long time

ARABIC

정

jeong/jung

Deep affection, affinity, connectedness
(not necessarily romantic)

KOREAN

Gjensynsglede

"goodbye happiness"
the joy of meeting someone you haven't seen in a long time

NORWEGIAN

gemas

A feeling of love or affection, the urge to squeeze someone because they are so cute

INDONESIAN

gadugi

Cooperative labour, working together for the common good

CHEROKEE

Freudentaumel

"joy swash"
being giddy or delirious with happiness

GERMAN

Arbejdsglaede

"work gladness"
Pleasure and satisfaction derived from work

DANISH

vakasteglok

Taking care of one's parents, 'in return', in recognition and gratitude for the care they took of us in the past

MWOTLAP
(VANATU)

静寂
Seijaku

Quiet (*sei*) tranquillity (*jaku*)
Silence, calm & serenity, especially in the midst of chaos

JAPANESE

靠譜
Kào pŭ

Reliable, responsible; able to do things without causing problems

CHINESE

ᐃᓄᖅᑲᑎᒌᑦᑎᐊᕐᓂᖅ
Inuuqatigiittiarniq

Being respectful of all people, healthy communities; neighbourliness; living in peace and harmony with others

INUKITUT
(Canadian Inuit)

leash

A valued condition of being in balance with the community and the wider world

MONGOLIAN

וְלָשׁ
shalev

Calm, peaceful, quiet, at ease

HEBREW

tarruru

Evening glow, dying down, peace of mind

NGARLUMA
(aboriginal)

น้ำใจ
nam jai

"water from the heart"
selfless generosity and kindness

THAI

關係
Guān xì

Cultivating relationships & reciprocal connections, social karma, generosity or an act of mutual assistance.

CHINESE

source: The Positive Lexicography Project by Dr Tim Lomas

Transgender Rights Are Spreading

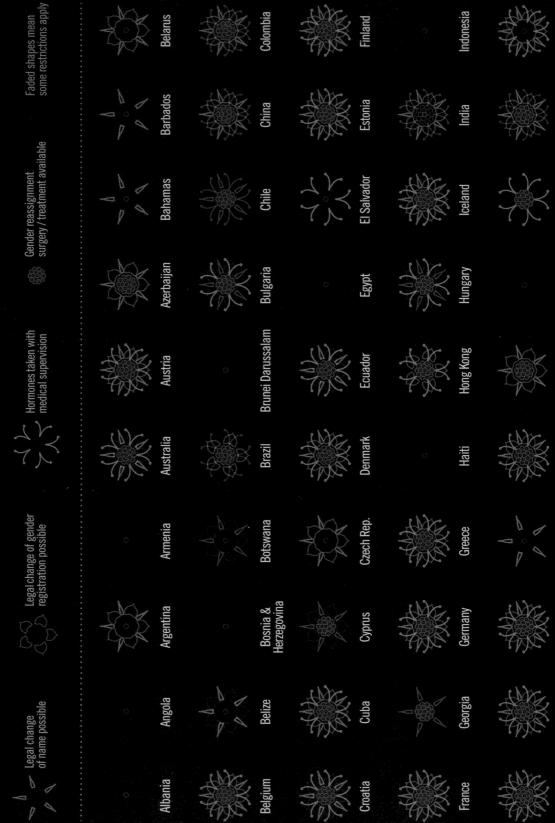

Legend:

- Legal change of name possible
- Legal change of gender registration possible
- Hormones taken with medical supervision
- Gender reassignment surgery / treatment available
- Faded shapes mean some restrictions apply

Albania
Angola
Argentina
Armenia
Australia
Austria
Azerbaijan
Bahamas
Barbados
Belarus

Belgium
Belize
Bosnia & Herzegovina
Botswana
Brazil
Brunei Darussalam
Bulgaria
Chile
China
Colombia

Croatia
Cuba
Cyprus
Czech Rep.
Denmark
Ecuador
Egypt
El Salvador
Estonia
Finland

France
Georgia
Germany
Greece
Haiti
Hong Kong
Hungary
Iceland
India
Indonesia

Ireland
Israel
Italy
Jamaica
Japan
Kazakhstan
Kenya
Kosovo
Kyrgyzstan
Latvia

Lithuania

Luxembourg

Malawi

Malaysia

Malta

Mexico

Moldova

Mongolia

Montenegro

Namibia

Nepal

Netherlands

New Caledonia

New Zealand

Nicaragua

Nigeria

N. Macedonia

Norway

Pakistan

Papua New Guinea

Peru

Philippines

Poland

Portugal

Puerto Rico

Romania

Russia

Saint Lucia

San Marino

Serbia

Singapore

Slovakia

Slovenia

Solomon Islands

South Africa

South Korea

Spain

Suriname

Sweden

Switzerland

Taiwan

Tajikistan

Tanzania

Thailand

Timor-Leste

Tonga

Trinidad & Tobago

Turkey

Uganda

Ukraine

United Kingdom

USA

Uzbekistan

Venezuela

Vietnam

Zambia

Zimbabwe

source: transrespect.org

Hundreds of New Vaccines Are in the Pipeline

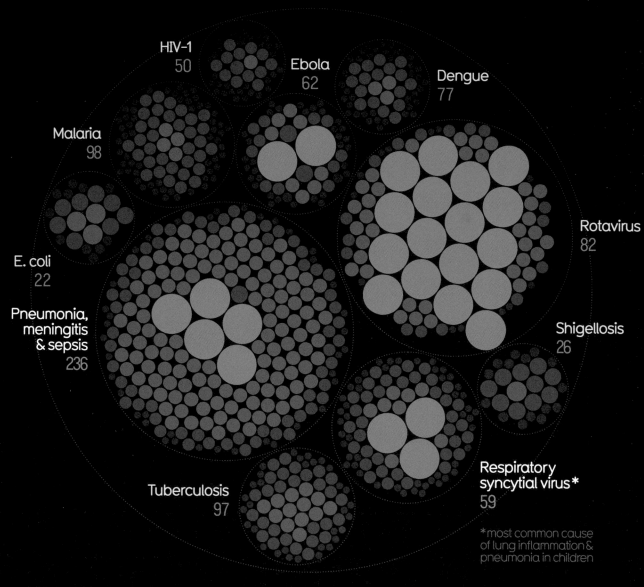

HIV-1
50

Ebola
62

Dengue
77

Malaria
98

Rotavirus
82

E. coli
22

Pneumonia,
meningitis
& sepsis
236

Shigellosis
26

Respiratory
syncytial virus*
59

Tuberculosis
97

*most common cause
of lung inflammation &
pneumonia in children

VACCINE TRIAL PHASES
average development time

stage

I   Is it safe for humans?
    2 yrs

II   Are there any side effects?
     2.5 yrs

III   Does it work in the real world?
      7.5 yrs

Approval
2 yrs

IV   Released, monitored for adverse effects
     lifelong

measles

530,000

chickenpox

4 million

250 thousand   200   150   100   50   0   0   50

sources: World Health Organization, EU Vaccine Initiative, Global Burden of Disease Collaborative Network, US Centers for Disease Control

Lives Saved by Vaccines in the Last 25+ Years
Global deaths from vaccine-preventable diseases

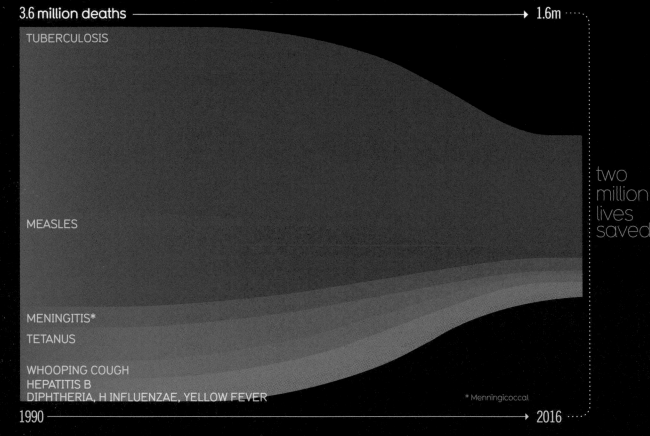

3.6 million deaths ────────────────→ 1.6m

TUBERCULOSIS

MEASLES

MENINGITIS*

TETANUS

WHOOPING COUGH
HEPATITIS B
DIPHTHERIA, H INFLUENZAE, YELLOW FEVER

* Menningicoccal

two
million
lives
saved

1990 ────────────────→ 2016

They Are a Great Economic Investment
For every dollar invested in lower-income countries

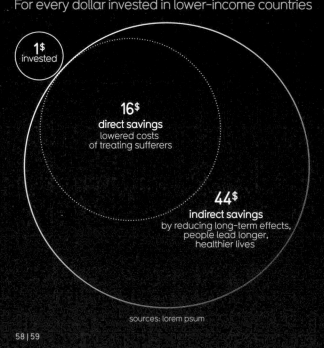

1$
invested

16$
direct savings
lowered costs
of treating sufferers

44$
indirect savings
by reducing long-term effects,
people lead longer,
healthier lives

sources: lorem psum

COVID Vaccines Save Millions of Lives
Estimated 75%-80% reduced death rate worldwide

11
thousand
COVID deaths
averted in the UK

millions
saved worldwide

sources: BBC, Public Health England

Indigenous Communities Safeguard the Forests of the World

Forest owned by native peoples has risen 40%

2002   **3.7** million km^2 **5.2** million km^2 2017

Good thing, because forests like these are storing
1,080 billion tonnes of CO2

Humanity's yearly CO2 emissions: 32bn

Deforestation emissions are much lower on these lands, meaning forests are now safer

Bolivia	Brazil	Colombia	Ecuador
-77%	-92%	-72%	-64%

sources: RightsandResources.org, ForestLivelihoods.org

Creative Ways to Deal with Our Emissions

Iceland Is Injecting Carbon Emissions Deep Underground
Forming minerals that last millions of years

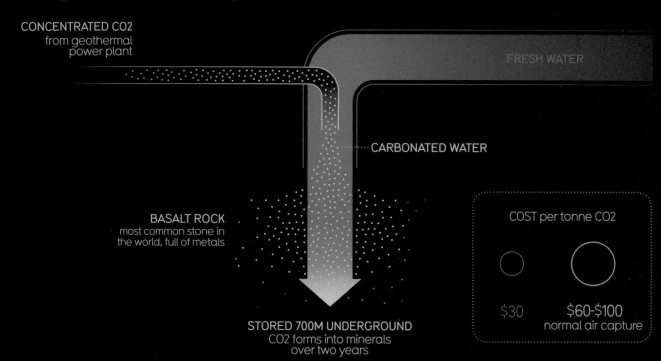

CONCENTRATED CO2
from geothermal
power plant

FRESH WATER

CARBONATED WATER

BASALT ROCK
most common stone in
the world, full of metals

COST per tonne CO2

$30 $60-$100
           normal air capture

STORED 700M UNDERGROUND
CO2 forms into minerals
over two years

sources: BBC, RTE

Home Methane Digesters Can Replace Inefficient Cookstoves

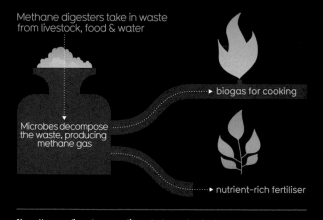

Methane digesters take in waste
from livestock, food & water

biogas for cooking

Microbes decompose
the waste, producing
methane gas

nutrient-rich fertiliser

If methane digesters continue to be adopted...

total global emissions

19 gigatonnes of CO2
emissions could be
avoided by 2050

source: Project Drawdown

Coral-Like Bioconcrete Generates Zero Emissions

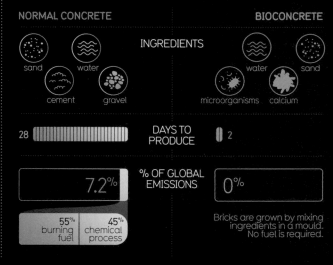

NORMAL CONCRETE   BIOCONCRETE

INGREDIENTS

sand   water   water   sand

cement   gravel   microorganisms   calcium

28 ||||||||||||||||||||||||||||| DAYS TO PRODUCE   2

7.2%   % OF GLOBAL EMISSIONS   0%

55%   45%
burning   chemical
fuel   process

Bricks are grown by mixing
ingredients in a mould.
No fuel is required.

sources: Wired UK, Biomason, WRI, Chatham House

'Bling without Sting' Storing CO2 as Diamonds

 carbon dioxide captured from the air

 high-pressure chemical reaction

 using wind & renewable energy

creates an
ECO-DIAMOND

each carat removes
20 tonnes
of CO2

EMISSIONS PER PERSON PER YEAR

 5 UK
7 CHINA & EU
13 CANADA
17 USA

The 'Whale Pump' Could Be the Ultimate Natural Carbon Sink

faecal plumes from whales
rich in nitrogen and iron

feed surface phytoplankton
microscopic algae

who capture 40% of our emissions
equivalent of 1.7 trillion trees

whales also accumulate
33 tonnes
of carbon in their bodies

each whale
$2
MILLION
in carbon capture

stored in the deep ocean when they die

all whales
$1
TRILLION
world wide

sources: Scientific American, International Monetary Fund

New Cookstoves Are Safer, Last Longer & Reduce Emissions

40%
of the world's population cook over open fires, using unhealthy fuels like...

 wood
 animal dung
 charcoal
 crop residues
 coal

smoke from these fuels has negative effects

deaths		emissions
HEART DISEASE	9.4m	2% to 5% global green-house gases
INDOOR AIR POLLUTION	4.3m	
DIABETES	1.6m	
ROAD ACCIDENTS	1.4m	

1.5 million households already use a new improved stove that cuts emissions by

95%

reduced smoke & soot means fewer deaths from air pollution

secondary oxygen intake forces gases & smoke back into flames, increasing efficiency

wood gas

solid fuel
wood pellets, not always easy to obtain

primary oxygen intake

sources: Project Drawdown, Scientific American, energypedia.info

Yay UK!

Biodiversity **Is Flourishing in the Thames**

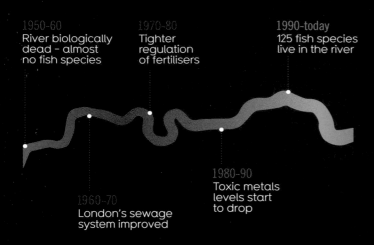

1950-60
River biologically
dead - almost
no fish species

1970-80
Tighter
regulation
of fertilisers

1990-today
125 fish species
live in the river

1960-70
London's sewage
system improved

1980-90
Toxic metals
levels start
to drop

sources: BBC, Zoological Society of London, Port of London Authority

UK Teen Pregnancies Hit a Recor
Births per 1,000 women aged 15-19

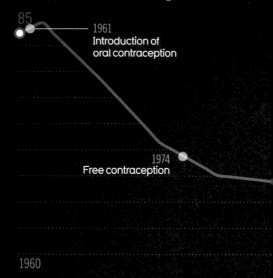

85

1961
Introduction of
oral contraception

1974
Free contraception

1960

UK's Carbon Emissions Are Falling Fast
Thanks to cleaner electricity and declining energy use

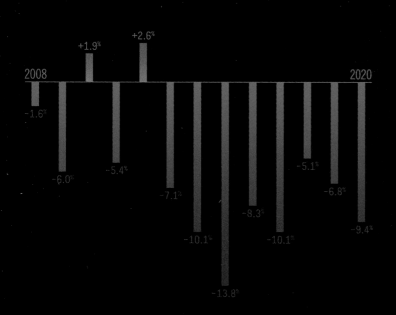

+1.9%

+2.6%

2008

2020

-1.6%

-6.0%

-5.4%

-7.1%

-8.3%

-5.1%

-10.1%

-10.1%

-6.8%

-9.4%

-13.8%

Coal Use **Is Being Cut, Fast**
% of energy mix

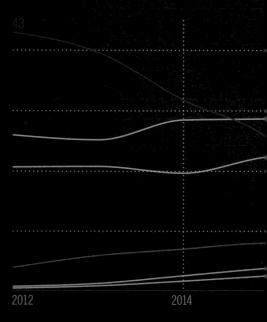

43

2012

2014

source: mygridGB

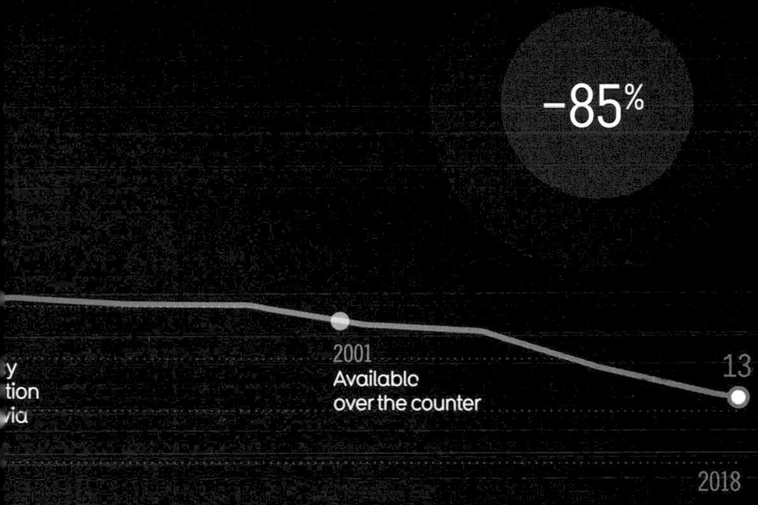

−85%

2001
Available
over the counter

13

2018

source: World Bank

Smoking in Pregnancy Down
% smokers at time of delivery

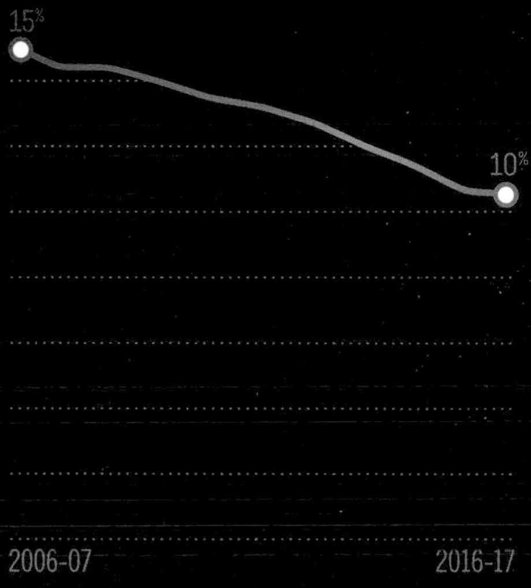

15%

10%

2006-07

2016-17

source: BBC

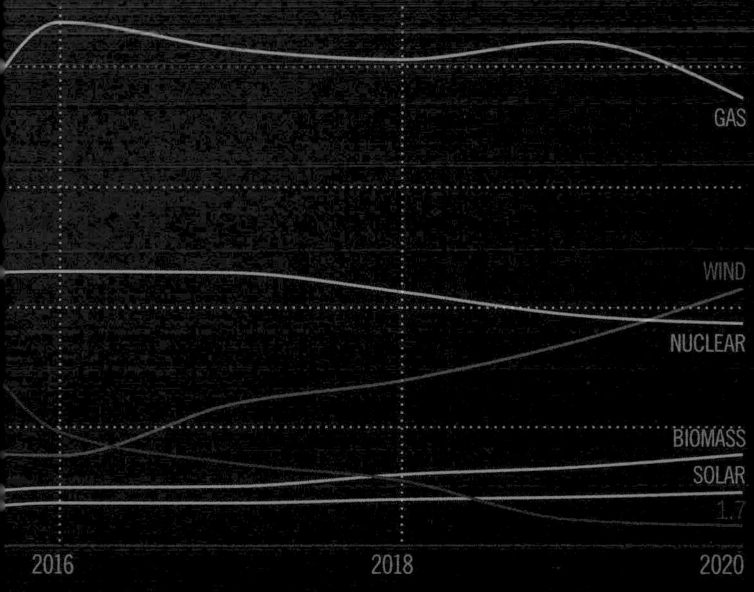

GAS

WIND

NUCLEAR

BIOMASS
SOLAR
1.7

2016

2018

2020

source: MyGridGB

Biggest Offshore Wind Farms
UK, Netherlands, Germany

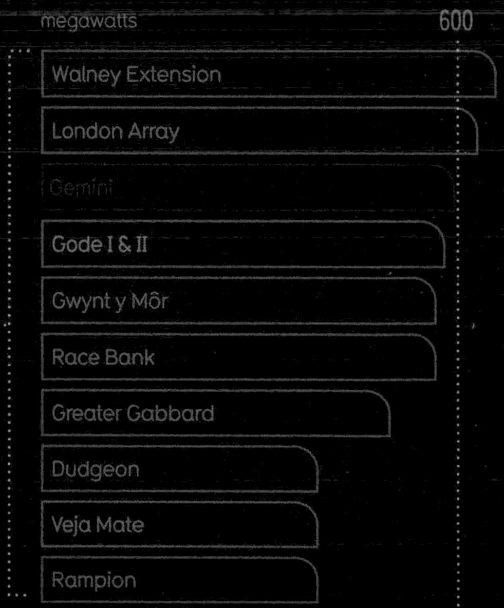

megawatts   600

| Walney Extension |
| London Array |
| Gemini |
| Gode I & II |
| Gwynt y Môr |
| Race Bank |
| Greater Gabbard |
| Dudgeon |
| Veja Mate |
| Rampion |

source: Guardian

Women

More Women Are in Parliament Around the World

Rwanda

60%

Bolivia

Andorra

Cuba

Sweden

40%

global average 25.2%

20%

11.7%

1997

2020

source: World Bank

There Have Never Been More Female CEOs
In the Fortune 500

2020

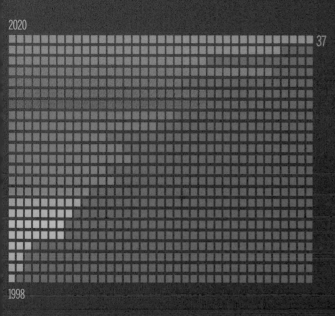

37

1998

source: Fortune

Women's Economic Freedom Is Protected Almost Everywhere

Women, Business & the Law Index
assigns a score based on laws that affect women's economic opportunities across 8 key areas

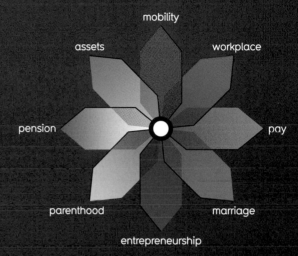

mobility

assets

workplace

pension

pay

parenthood

marriage

entrepreneurship

More US Women Are Moving into Science, Tech, Engineering & Math

1970

2019

70% in STEM jobs

social sciences

50%

mathematics

life & physical sciences

30%

computing

engineering

10%

source: United States Census Bureau

Overall Freedom Score by Country

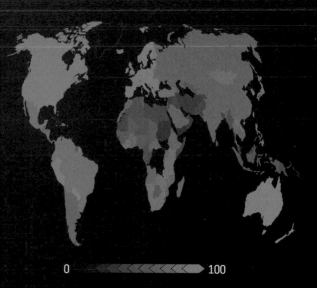

0

100

source: World Bank

Can Next-Gen Nuclear Energy Get Us to Carbon Zero?

PROS

zero carbon
global-scale electricity with no greenhouse gas emissions

consistent energy
backup when intermittent power like wind can't deliver

established industry
already generates ~10% of the world's electricity

small footprint
very little land required vs vast space for solar & wind

quickest route
slash CO2, decarbonise in years not centuries

need it now
difficult to imagine net carbon zero by 2050 without it

CONS

radioactive waste
average plant creates 27 tonnes yearly, active for 24,000 years

hugely expensive
More than $10bn to build. Can't compete with renewables on $$$

old, aging tech
many reactors are 30-40 years old & beset with reliability issues

big fear
the public is afraid of nuclear – accidents, waste, weapons...

reactors slow to build
takes 6-10 years – we'd need 100s now to replace fossil fuels

regulatory holdups
approving, insuring and testing new plants is a massive block

RESPONSES

waste storage is possib
nations like Sweden have so established storage of pluto

some fear is irrational
nuclear is much safer than c (kills 500K a year from polluti

Current State of Nuclear Energy Around the World

UK France
South Korea
China UAE
Finland Russia
India Turkey
Argentina

TOSHIBA Spain
Germany
Japan
Italy Belgium
Westinghouse eDF
Switzerland

436 reactors

31 countries

50 more being built

several
countries & **companies** phasing ou

Next-Gen Nuclear

ADVANCED REACTOR TYPES

dominant tech

PRESSURISED WATER REACTOR

Super-heated water pumped into radioactive core. Resulting heat turns an electric turbine.

✗ CAN OVERHEAT & MELT DOWN, SO SAFETY A BIG OPERATIONAL COST

✗ INEFFICIENT - ONLY 1% OF POTENTIAL ENERGY HARVESTED

emerging tech

MOLTEN SALT REACTOR

Nuclear fuel dissolved in liquid salt at 600-700°C & circulated through the core

✔ VERY SAFE - REACTION SLOWS DOWN AUTOMATICALLY AS FUEL IS USED UP

✔ CAN RUN ON NUCLEAR WASTE OR SUPERABUNDANT THORIUM

experimental tech

TRAVELLING WAVE REACTOR

Simultaneously burns fuel & creates new fuel creating self-sustaining 'burn wave' of energy

✔ RUNAWAY REACTIONS IMPOSSIBLE

✔ NO REFUELLING NEEDED EVERY 2 YEARS

✔ RECYCLING! USES ITS OWN WASTE AS FUEL

problematic tech

FAST BREEDER REACTOR

Reycles the fuel repeatedly at very fast rates extracting more and more energy

✔ CAN RUN OFF PLUTONIUM NUCLEAR WASTE

✗ REQUIRES WASTE TO BE CONVERTED INTO AN EXPENSIVE METAL ALLOY

✗ THIS METAL COULD BE STOLEN OR DIVERTED

prototype tech

PEBBLE-BED HIGH-TEMP REACTOR

Fuel is packed Into tennis-ball-sized spheres (pebbles) instead of fuel rods

✔ SAFE - PEBBLES BLOCK RADIOACTIVITY

✔ CAN BE CONTINUALLY FUELLED

✔ HIGH TEMPERATURE GENERATES EVEN MORE ELECTRICITY

SIZE VARIATIONS

SMALL MODULAR REACTORS

Compact, factory-produced nuclear modules that can be combined to increase output

50-300 megawatts
(mid-sized town)

✔ LESS UPFRONT $$$ NEEDED

✔ STANDARDISED DESIGN, SO CHEAPER & QUICKER TO BUILD & MASS PRODUCE

✔ SMALL CORES LESS HOT, UNLIKELY TO OVERHEAT

MICROREACTORS

Even smaller, super-portable power sources that can be transported by truck, ship or plane

1-20 megawatts
(small town)

✔ CAN RUN FOR 10 YEARS WITHOUT REFUELLING

✔ IDEAL FOR REMOTE LOCATION OR LOWER-INCOME NATIONS

✗ REQUIRE HIGHER-CONCENTRATION URANIUM FUEL SO NEEDS SPECIAL SUPPLY

Canada China Russia UK USA
all building SMRs

sources: Yale School of Environment, New York Times, Asia Times, UIS Office of Nuclear Energy,

Nuclear Fusion Could Supply Clean, Limitless Power

The Holy Grail of energy - if only we can make it happen

HOW IT WORKS

existing nuclear reactors create energy by splitting atoms apart (**fission**)

fusion smashes atoms together to reproduce the energy of the stars

creating a 'miniature sun' that generates more energy than it consumes

the hydrogen in a glass of water is enough energy for one person's lifetime

zero emissions, no carbon, no green-house gases, no global heating

much less **radioactive waste** vs traditional fission reactors (100s of years vs 1,000s)

very safe - there's no chance of melt down; plasma just cools if disrupted

IT'S NOT EASY

the fuel must be heated up to unbelievably high temperatures

MILLION DEGREES CENTIGRADE

- 15 — temperature at the centre of the sun
- 20
- 40
- 60
- 80
- 100 — minimum temperature required for deuterium-tritium* fusion
- 120
- 140
- 150 — operating temperature at ITER

* alternate forms of hydrogen (isotopes) required for fusion

the heat turns the fuel into a plasma

an energized mix of charged particles

a violently unstable state

must somehow be contained & controlled

WHEN IS IT COMING?

new ultra-powerful superconducting magnets

CREATE VASTLY STRONGER CONTAINMENT FIELDS

innovative liquid nitrogen cooling processes

MUCH CHEAPER THAN CURRENT LIQUID HELIUM

5-10

years is finally a credible ETA

AFTER 50 YEARS OF FALSE STARTS

novel materials able to withstand the plasma

REDUCED-ACTIVATION STEEL & TUNGSTEN

next-gen fusion techniques already emerging

STELLARATORS & LATTICE-CONFINEMENT

International Thermonuclear Experimental Reactor
ITER is the world's largest fusion megaproject

Paris

Cadarache

IN PROVENCE
SOUTHERN FRANCE

EXTRAORDINARY
COLLABORATION
BETWEEN

35
NATIONS

including
European Union
China
India
Japan
Russia
S. Korea
USA

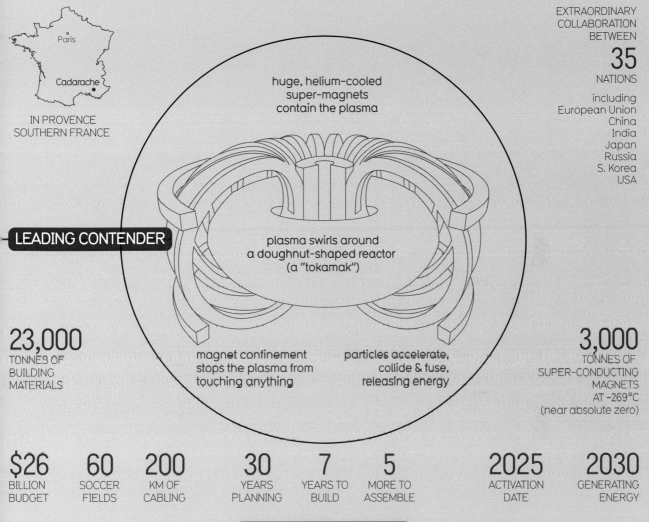

huge, helium-cooled
super-magnets
contain the plasma

LEADING CONTENDER

plasma swirls around
a doughnut-shaped reactor
(a "tokamak")

23,000
TONNES OF
BUILDING
MATERIALS

magnet confinement
stops the plasma from
touching anything

particles accelerate,
collide & fuse,
releasing energy

3,000
TONNES OF
SUPER-CONDUCTING
MAGNETS
AT −269°C
(near absolute zero)

$26	**60**	**200**	**30**	**7**	**5**	**2025**	**2030**
BILLION BUDGET	SOCCER FIELDS	KM OF CABLING	YEARS PLANNING	YEARS TO BUILD	MORE TO ASSEMBLE	ACTIVATION DATE	GENERATING ENERGY

CREDIBLE ALTERNATIVE

Field Reverse Configuration (FRC) using hydrogen-boron as a fuel

hydrogen-boron
produces 3-4x
more energy

with virtually
zero waste

but requires
extraordinary
temperatures

5.4 BILLION
DEGREES **!**
but actually feasible

in FRC, the hotter
the plasma,
the more stable

complete
opposite of a
tokamak

sources: World Economic Forum, EcoWatch, New York Times, BBC, Wikipedia, Bill Gates "How to Avoid A Climate Disaster"

At Least 100 Towns & Cities Now Get Most of Their Energy from Renewables

Reporting more than 70% green energy

S. America

Nova Odessa
Alcaldía de Córdoba
Tatuí
Campinas
Santos
Águas de São Pedro
São Gonçalo
Lorena
Salvador
Ibagué
Brusque
São Bento do Sapucaí
Belém
Santiago de Cali
Quito
Temuco
Capivari
Uberlândia
Palmas
Cajamar
Florianópolis
Aracaju
São José do Rio Preto
Bogotá
Medellín
Campos de Goytacazes
Niterói
Jaboatão dos Guararapes
Brotas
Estâ de IT
São Caetano
Angra dos Reis
São José dos Campos
Extrema
Curitiba
São João da Boa Vist
Aparecida
Brasília
Vitória
Goiânia
Fernandópo
Vinhedo
Belo Horizonte
Asunción
Birigui
Mairiporã
Montes Claros
Cabreúva
Caxias do Sul
Maceió
Canoas
Assis
Cerquilho
Limeira
Guaratinguetá

Colombian city already boasts 28% geotherm 66% hydro.

Capital of Paraguay is entirely powered by the vast Itaipu & Yacyretá hydrodams.

population

Asia

This South Korea city has pledged to 100% renewable energy by 2045.

Inje

North America

Vancouver

N. Vancouver

Seattle

Burlington

Prince George, BC

Became first city in the USA to run entirely on renewables in 2015.

Montreal

León de los Aldamas

Chorrera   Aspen

Winnipeg

Eugene

This Colorado town is 100% renewable, including 53% wind!

Oceania

Kapiti Coast

Auckland

Hobart

Wellington

Africa

Nakuru

Bangangté

Foumban

Quelimane

Dar es Salaam

Nairobi

Kisumu

Harare

Extensive solar power has been developed to counter Zimbabwe's frequent power cuts.

Powered by the city's renewable energy company.

Europe

Fafe

Gladsaxe

Arendal

Bærum

Basel

Zürich

Braga

Moita

Alba-Iulia

Porto

Stockholm

Akureyri

Cascais

Bolzano

Reykjavík

Lausanne

Oslo

Oristano

Nyon

All electricity comes from hydro & geothermal. Aiming to have all carbon-free transport by 2040.

source: Carbon Disclosure Project

Chad -56%
Burundi -60%
Central African Rep. -60%
DRC -63%
Nigeria -67%
Sierra Leone -71%
Turkmenistan -73%
Togo -76%
Uzbekistan -79%
Afghanistan -82%
Cambodia -87%
Mon… -89%

Guinea-Bissau -60%
Guyana -66%
Somalia -64%
Zimbabwe -69%
Tonga -72%
Kiribati -73%
Swaziland -76%
Haiti -79%
Ethiopia -82%
Saint Vincent and the Grenadines -86%
Fiji -89%

Niger -66%
Paraguay -67%
Cameroon -67%
Uganda -69%
Zambia -72%
Mali -74%
Melanesia -77%
Laos -80%
United States -82%
Jamaica -86%
Ecu… -89%

Mauritania -70%
Equatorial Guinea -78%
Djibouti -70%
Sudan -70%
Benin -72%
Mozambique -74%
Congo -77%
Channel Islands -80%
Argentina -83%
Moldova -86%
Den… -89%

São Tomé and Príncipe -72%
Micronesia -73%
Lesotho -73%
South Sudan -73%
Guinea -74%
Burkina Faso -77%
Rwanda -80%
Gabon -83%
Honduras -87%
Cur… -89%

Angola -75%
Trinidad and Tobago -75%
Comoros -75%
Papua New Guinea -75%
Ghana -76%
Malawi -78%
Tajikistan -80%
India -83%
Panama -86%
We Sah -89%

Cote d'Ivoire -78%
Tanzania -78%
Pakistan -78%
Bolivia -78%
Uruguay -78%
Liberia -79%
South Africa -80%
Madagascar -84%
Australia -87%
Net -89%

World -80%
Kenya -80%
Philippines -81%
Azerbaijan -81%
Botswana -82%
Gambia -82%
Suriname -82%
Myanmar -84%
Vietnam -87%
Kyr -89%

Yemen -84%
Aruba -85%
Namibia -85%
Eritrea -85%
New Zealand -85%
Armenia -85%
Senegal -86%
Solomon Islands -86%
United Kingdom -87%

Samoa -88%
Timor -88%
Polynesia -88%
Bahamas -88%
Guatemala -88%
Colombia -89%
United States Virgin Islands -88%
Georgia -88%
Cape Verde -87%
Car… -89%

Kazakhstan -90%
Mexico -90%
Belize -90%
Switzerland -90%
Sweden -90%
Bangladesh -90%
Palestine -90%
Vanuatu -90%
Algeria -90%
Nep… -90%

ps in infant and child mortality since 1950

Iraq -90%	Mongolia -91%	Jordan -93%	Ukraine -93%	France -94%	Finland -95%	Saudi Arabia -96%	Japan -97%	Réunion -98%
Bhutan -91%	Brazil -92%	Bulgaria -93%	French Guiana -93%	Turkey -94%	Russia -95%	Montenegro -95%	Estonia -97%	Mayotte -98%
Indonesia -91%	Romania -92%	Israel -93%	Tunisia -94%	Ireland -94%	Egypt -95%	Qatar -95%	Italy -96%	Portugal -98%
Dominican Republic -90%	Malta -92%	El Salvador -92%	Saint Lucia -93%	Thailand -94%	Martinique -95%	Iran -95%	Bosnia and Herzegovina -96%	Belarus -97%
Syria -91%	Guam -92%	Puerto Rico -92%	Brunei -94%	Hungary -94%	Cyprus -95%	Poland -95%	Taiwan -96%	Hong Kong -98%
Peru -90%	Norway -92%	Barbados -92%	Mauritius -93%	Sri Lanka -94%	Malaysia -95%	Czech Republic -95%	Bahrain -97%	Maldives -98%
Venezuela -91%	North Korea -92%	Libya -92%	Iceland -93%	N. Macedonia -94%	Cuba -95%	Austria -95%	Croatia -96%	South Korea -98%
Slovenia -91%	Grenada -92%	Albania -92%	Belgium -93%	Greece -94%	Chile -95%	Guadeloupe -96%	Spain -97%	Oman -97%
Lebanon -90%	Antigua and Barbuda -92%	New Caledonia -92%	Costa Rica -93%	China -94%	Germany -94%	Kuwait -95%	Macao -96%	Singapore -97%
Seychelles -90%	Nicaragua -92%	Serbia -93%	Luxembourg -94%	Slovakia -94%	Latvia -95%	French Polynesia -96%	Lithuania -97%	United Arab Emirates -98%

source: Our World in Data

How to get the world to NET CARBON ZERO * by 2050

*net carbon zero

Doesn't necessarily mean zero emissions. There will still be some emissions — though massively reduced. But CO_2 capture, offsetting and other methods will mean the overall emissions in the global or national system will be zero.

DEEP DECARBONISATION
80–100% reduction
in global emissions

TWO ROUTES

100% renewables
wind & solar
supported by energy
storage, new grids
& transmission
systems

mix
wind & solar +
nuclear, geothermal
& limited fossil fuels

reduce
emissions

increase
efficiency

decarbonise
energy

boost
carbon sinks

MAYBE

carbon
capture

Where Do Our Emissions Come From?

source: Our World in Data

INDUSTRY 29.4%

iron & steel
7.2%

chemical & petrochemical production
5.8%

greenhouse gases can be produced as a byproduct of chemical processes like the manufacturing of fertilisers, pharmaceuticals, refrigerants, alongside oil and gas extraction, etc.

other industries
10.6%

cement
3.0%

food & tobacco
1.0%

digital tech
3.7%

servers, networks, computers, screens, devices (manufacture & use)

metals
0.7%

paper, printing
0.6%

machinery
0.5%

LAND USE 20.1%

livestock & manure
5.8%

with agriculture it's mostly methane from cattle burps & excrement, plus rice growing & other water-logged soils that contribute to emissions

fertilizers
4.1%

crop-burning
3.5%

deforestation
2.2%

agricultural machinery
1.7%

cropland
1.4%

rice growing
1.3%

residential
0.9%

cars & trucks
11.9%

BUILDINGS
17.5%

includes emissions for
lighting, energy use, and
both heating & cooling
(air conditioning)

commercial
6.6%

TRANSPORT
16.2%

aviation
1.9%

ships
1.7%

rail
0.4%

pipelines
0.3%

other fuels
7.8%

oil & natural gas leaks & losses
3.9%

landfills
1.9%

ENERGY
13.6%

WASTE
2.2%

coal mining leaks & losses
1.9%

biomass, nuclear
& pumped hydro

wastewater
& sewage
1.3%

How to Halve Emissions by 2030

ENERGY
DECARBONISE ELECTRICITY
−6.2%

increased solar power
−2.2%

widespread wind energy
−2.7%

other renewables
−1.3%

LAND USE
SUPPORT CARBON SINKS
−6.5%

land restoration
−0.6%

sustainable agriculture techniques
−1.3%

halting deforestation, planting trees
forest management
−4.6%

BUILDINGS
ELECTRIFY HEATING
−9.6%

low-carbon heating & cooking
−3.9%

low-carbon construction
−1.8%

automated thermostats and lighting
−0.8%

retro-fitting buildings
adding better insulation, ventilation, smart windows, LED lighting, etc.
−2.7%

other
−4.5%

reduced food waste
−1.3%

plant-based diets
−3.3%

EMISSIONS REDUCED **27.6** gigatonnes of CO2e

CO2e = carbon dioxide equivalent = a way of combining all greenhouse gas emissions in one measure

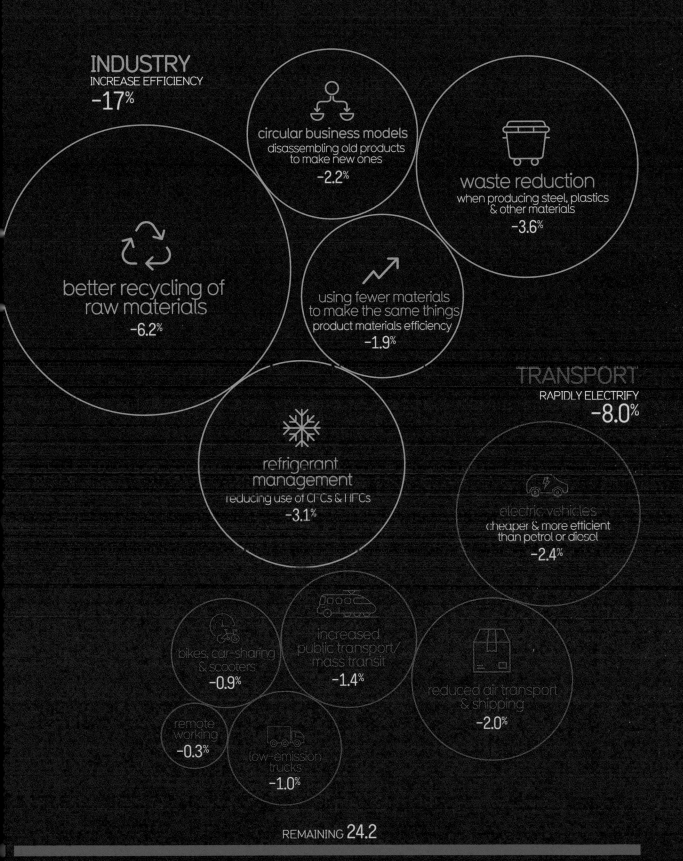

INDUSTRY
INCREASE EFFICIENCY
-17%

circular business models
disassembling old products
to make new ones
-2.2%

waste reduction
when producing steel, plastics
& other materials
-3.6%

better recycling of
raw materials
-6.2%

using fewer materials
to make the same things
product materials efficiency
-1.9%

TRANSPORT
RAPIDLY ELECTRIFY
-8.0%

refrigerant
management
reducing use of CFCs & HFCs
-3.1%

electric vehicles
cheaper & more efficient
than petrol or diesel
-2.4%

bikes, car-sharing
& scooters
-0.9%

increased
public transport/
mass transit
-1.4%

reduced air transport
& shipping
-2.0%

remote
working
-0.3%

low-emission
trucks
-1.0%

REMAINING **24.2**

sources: Our World in Data, Project Drawdown, ECOFYS, Exponential Climate Action Roadmap, IEA

Carbon Zero by 2050 Project Plan

ENERGY

renewables!
rapid upscale of renewable carbon-free electricity
(solar, wind, wave, geothermal)

▸174

install advanced smart- & micro-grids
so we can use the variable power of renewables

develop grid-scale electrical storage
big-ass batteries, basically

improve efficiency
so much energy is lost through inefficiency

extend electricity transmission networks
especially high voltage both above- and underground

expand clean 'firm' power
nuclear, hydro, geothermal

increase biofuel & hydrogen use
adding carbon capture

retire fossil-fuel power plants early

burn waste & convert it to power, capturing emissions
waste-to-energy

reduce individual consumption in richer nations

TRANSPORT

electric vehicles dominate the roads
+ widespread charging grids

 passenger cars

 light/med. trucks

buses

phase out fossil-fuel vehicles

reduce vehicle use, adding diverse alternatives
public transport, scooters, bikes, car & taxi pooling, walkable cities, high-speed rail, pooled ride-hailing

taxes on inefficient fuel & vehicles

higher fuel economy & emissions standards

more efficient aviation

switch to advanced biofuels
to power 'electrification-resistant' trucks, ships, and airplanes

 long haul trucks

 aircraft

 container ships

BUILDINGS

electrification
heating, stoves & furnaces

zero-carbon buildings go mainstream

aggressive electrical appliance standards
to increase efficiency & lighten demand on the grid

establish & police higher energy-efficiency standards

supply carbon-neutral fuels for older buildings
that cannot be retro-fitted

increase air-conditioning efficiency
could reduce overall building energy demand by 45% global

LAND USE

methane (natural gas) capture and destruction
landfill-captured methane used to produce electricity

▸228

reforestation
even more tree planting and land restoration

▸126

enhance sustainable land sinks in agriculture
sinks absorb CO2 naturally

improve rice production
flooded rice paddies produce large quantities of methane

agriculture sector globally on track to store more carbon than it emits
agroforestry & precision agriculture widely adopted

enhance land protection
increases natural carbon storehouses in soils

 land

grasslands

 wetlands

 peatlands

plant-rich diets
widespread adoption of low-carbon diets

height = impact
shaded = special difficulty
v. order = priority

INDUSTRY

new efficiency standards
help heavy industries to reach
max efficiency

switch from coal & natural gas to electricity, biofuels
& other sustainable alternatives

(re) design industrial facilities to reduce waste

reduce non-CO2 emissions
nitrous oxides, methane, etc.

all construction carbon neutral
or even stores CO2

industrial carbon capture, transport & storage (CCS)

decarbonise & electrify cement, steel & chemical processes

all companies adopt circular business models

fix refrigerants
flourinated 'F-gases' from airconditioners are potent GHGs
develop, promote & use alternatives

INVESTMENT

fund new carbon-free tech to ensure cheap, scaleable & widespread rollout in the years ahead

 next-gen nuclear ▸066

 geothermal

 hydrogen & ammonia combustion turbines

 cheap long-duration energy storage ▸144

 biomass & natural gas power plants with CO2 capture

carbon capture
storing industrial CO2 and/ or sucking CO2 from the atmosphere to store it underground
or using it to resynthesise fuels
▸214

 circular economy
where products & materials are sustainably designed & made to be reused or recycled, rather than dumped
▸140

POLICY

global 'carbon pricing'
catch-all term for taxes & credits to
• make carbon-emitting things more expensive
• disencourage fossil fuel production & use
• incentivise renewable tech & infrastructure
so new tech can compete against subsidised fossil tech

govt-backed financing, investment & regulatory support

international co-operation secures strong global climate agreement & roadmap
The Paris Agreement shows that it is possible
▸114

implement & support green new deals in every country

enact subsidies on renewable energy, green industries & climate tech

dramatically increase clean-energy R&D funding
+ incentives for innovation adoption & export of new tech

EQUITY

ensure climate finance flows to the Global South
alternative term for 'third' or 'developing' world

created just 8% of global GHGs

new jobs & training for displaced workers

government support for those affected

bring indigenous peoples into decision-making
their knowledge already protects forests & ecosystems
▸059

sources: New York Times, Zero Carbon Action Plan 2020,
Net Zero America (Princeton), How to Avoid a Climate Disaster (Bill Gates, 2020),
Project Drawdown, Our World in Data, Sitra, XCAR, ECOFYS, Exponential Climate Action Roadmap, IEA

What can we do personally?

We need to get average yearly global emissions per person down
to 2.1 tonnes CO2e

2050 TARGET 2.1	**CURRENT AVERAGE** 4.8	**5.3 UK**	**7.0 EU**	**CHINA** 7.2	

16.3 **AUSTRALIA**

CANADA 13.5

USA 16.6

Genuinely Impactful Actions

TONNES OF CO2e
SAVED PER YEAR

	0.5	1.0	1.5	2.0	
drop the car			bus, train, bike, walk		-2.4
take fewer flights			per one roundtrip trans-atlantic trip		-1.6
purchase green energy					-1.4
buy a more efficient car		with better fuel economy & maintenance			-1.2
get an electric car		still emits emissions via manufacture & energy usage			-1.2
switch to a plant-based diet	vegan ideal, vegetarian helps too				-0.8
hybrid car					-0.4
reduce food waste					-0.37
plant a tree					-0.3
wash clothes in cold water					-0.25
reduce meat					-0.23
hang clothes to dry					-0.21
recycling					-0.21
more efficient home heating	smart thermostats are the way to go				-0.18
change lightbulbs to LEDs					-0.1
talk to teens	establishing life-long habits are crucial	teens can catalyse other family members to act	plus they get it!		∞

source: 'The climate mitigation gap' (Wynes and Nicholas), Environmental Research Letters 201

Getting the USA to Carbon Zero by 2050

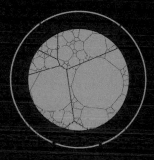

affordable
less than 1% of GDP required
per year to transition

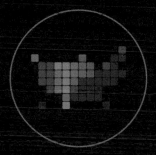

feasible
the technology already exists
– and is getting better

starting now
needs to happen now to lay
groundwork & infrastructure

working together
everyone participating – individuals,
corporations, government, institutions

The USA Is Ripe for Solar & Wind Power

Potential utility-scale solar energy capacity per state
(terawatt hours)

Receives more sunshine than Germany

Despite shorter days, Alaska is a suprisingly sunny state

Southern sun-belt states are drenched in potential solar power

Texas land space & sun could make it a solar powerhouse

State	TWh
Maine	1,104
Alaska	8,283
Wisconsin	5,097
Vermont	56
N. Hampshire	61
Washington	1,772
Idaho	3,960
Montana	8,199
N. Dakota	9,739
Minnesota	10,826
Illinois	8,195
Michigan	5,266
New York	1,545
Mass.	100
Oregon	3,766
Nevada	8,639
Wyoming	5,734
S. Dakota	10,013
Iowa	7,021
Indiana	4,975
Ohio	3,713
Pennsylvania	610
New Jersey	484
Connecticut	27
Rhode Island	15
California	9,102
Utah	5,215
Colorado	10,282
Nebraska	9,280
Missouri	5,366
Kentucky	1,850
W. Virginia	56
Virginia	1,910
Maryland	615
Delaware	287
Arizona	11,939
New Mexico	16,390
Kansas	14,532
Arkansas	5,105
Tennessee	2,276
N. Carolina	4,301
S. Carolina	2,789
Oklahoma	9,392
Louisiana	4,170
Mississippi	5,008
Alabama	3,743
Georgia	5,535
Hawaii	42
Texas	39,288
Florida	5,210

Potential onshore wind energy capacity per state (terawatt hours)

The Great Plains states have the fastest wind speeds so lots of energy to harvest

Ringed states have massive offshore wind potential

In more tropical states, air rises upward so there's little energy for turbines.

Texas's vast land area means lots of space for turbines

State	TWh
Maine	29
Alaska	1,373
Wisconsin	255
Vermont	9
N. Hampshire	8
Washington	47
Idaho	44
Montana	2,746
N. Dakota	2,534
Minnesota	1,429
Illinois	649
Michigan	144
New York	64
Mass.	3
Oregon	69
Nevada	21
Wyoming	1,654
S. Dakota	2,902
Iowa	1,724
Indiana	378
Ohio	129
Pennsylvania	10
New Jersey	0
Connecticut	0
Rhode Island	0
California	90
Utah	32
Colorado	1,096
Nebraska	3,011
Missouri	690
Kentucky	0
W. Virginia	6
Virginia	5
Maryland	4
Delaware	0
Arizona	31
New Mexico	1,399
Kansas	3,102
Arkansas	27
Tennessee	1
N. Carolina	2
S. Carolina	1
Oklahoma	1,522
Louisiana	1
Mississippi	0
Alabama	0
Georgia	0
Hawaii	12
Texas	5,552
Florida	0

source: US Renewable Energy Technical Potentials, Lopez et al. (2012)

Total Potential Solar Energy
282,845
terawatt hours

Potential Onshore Wind Energy
32,780

US yearly
electricity
use
4,127

Netzero Timeline

sector	what	today	2030	2050	
electric vehicles (INCREASE)	personal electric cars	1.6m	50m	300m	with all cars electric, US energy consumption drops by 13%
	% of new sales	2%	30-50%	100%	
	% of total cars	0.4%	6-17%	61-96%	battery costs expected to decrease 1,000% by 2030
	public charging points	90,000 +17,000 fast chargers*	3-5m +120,000 fast chargers	18m +720,000 fast chargers	* fast charger = 240-mile range for 30m charge
	electric trucks & buses	63,000	1,000,000	2,500,000+	all electric or hydrogen-cell power
	% of new sales	not clear	15%	80%	
homes (SWITCH)	heated by electric pumps	10-12m	25-30m	130m	
	% of total homes	5%	10-23%	80-100%	100% electric induction hobs
carbon-free electricity	share of energy (INCREASE)	37%	70-85%	98%+	for 100% renewables
	solar power	65GW	300GW	1.5TW	
	wind power	100GW	300GW	4.2TW	1m km² +64,000 km² offshore
	investment	$140bn	$810bn	$3.4tr	
power lines	new transmission lines (INCREASE)	not yet	195,000 GW/km	unclear but lots	extra demand will require new power lines
	power capacity (INCREASE)	not yet	+60%	+350%	about 75GW per year added
	investment	not yet	$530bn	$2.5tr	

power grids

grid battery capacity	23GW		100GW	
electric grid flexibility	n/a		+5–10%	+40%–60% *(because solar & wind is intermittent, not constant)*
batteries	0.9GW		5–15GW	150–180GW *(6-hour batteries to support the grid)*

alternative energies

BUILD hydrogen	not yet		3 EXAJOULES	8–19 EXAJOULES
BUILD biomass	33m ton/year		80m ton/year	620m ton/year
MAINTAIN existing nuclear	keep nuclear plants going		keep nuclear plans going	50% retired
BUILD new advanced nuclear	n/a		10–260GW	500GW+ *(250x1GW reactors (or 3,800 small reactors))*

fossil fuels

decrease as energy source	n/a		–75%	–90%
ELIMINATE coal	700 mines		200 mines	all mines shut
DECREASE natural gas	n/a		2–30%	–65%++

carbon capture

BUILD nationwide pipeline & storage network	not yet		begin construction	21,000–25,000 km²
gigatons per year captured	not yet		0.25	1.7–4.2 *(will lower emissions by 1 GT/year)*
reforestation	1 million hectares/year		1.3 million hectares/year	20–40 m hectares/year

jobs INCREASE

% of workforce in energy industry	1.5%		+3%	+300% *(4.5% of workforce in energy industry)*
extra jobs	not yet		+3 million	+5 million

sources: International Energy Agency, Bloomberg, Zero Carbon Action Plan 2020, Net Zero America (Princeton), New York Times

Net Zero Costs to 2030
$billions

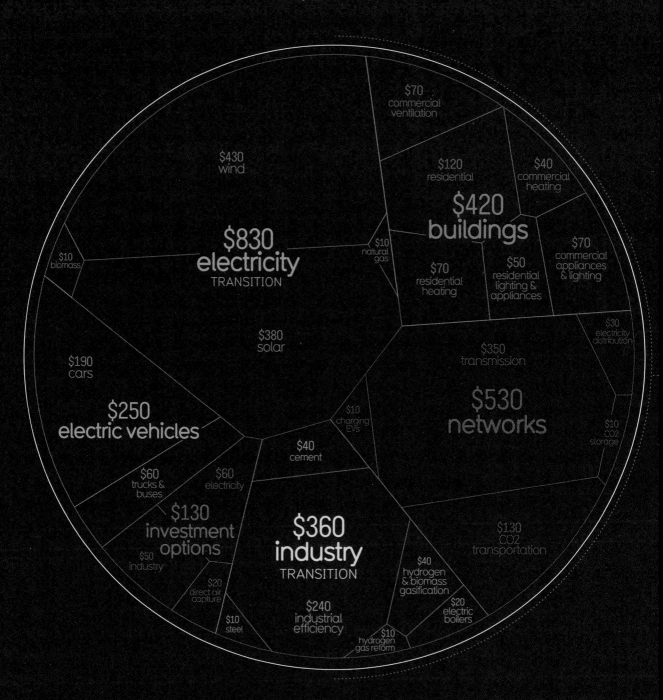

$70 commercial ventilation

$430 wind

$120 residential

$40 commercial heating

$830 electricity TRANSITION

$10 natural gas

$420 buildings

$70 commercial appliances & lighting

$10 biomass

$70 residential heating

$50 residential lighting & appliances

$380 solar

$30 electricity distribution

$190 cars

$350 transmission

$250 electric vehicles

$10 charging EVs

$530 networks

$10 CO2 storage

$40 cement

$60 trucks & buses

$60 electricity

$130 investment options

$360 industry TRANSITION

$130 CO2 transportation

$50 industry

$40 hydrogen & biomass gasification

$20 direct air capture

$20 electric boilers

$10 steel

$240 industrial efficiency

$10 hydrogen gas reform

source: Net Zero America (Princeton)

Comparison Costs
$trillions

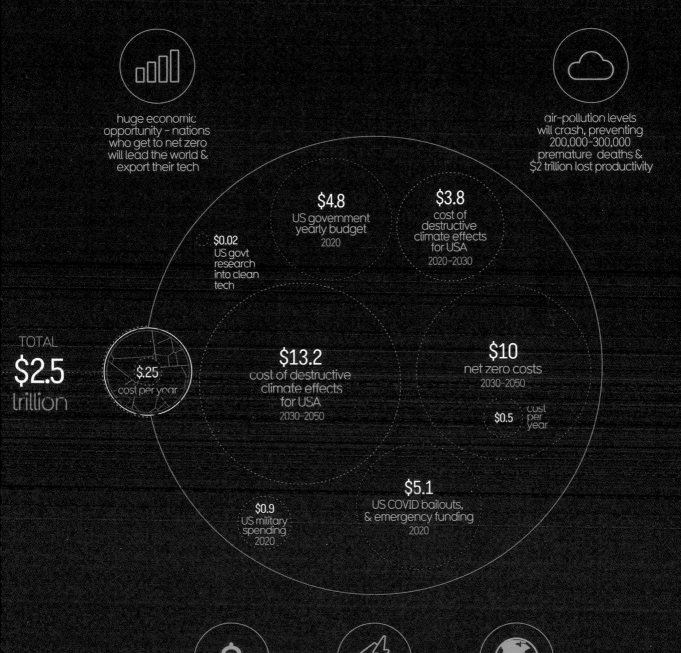

huge economic opportunity - nations who get to net zero will lead the world & export their tech

air-pollution levels will crash, preventing 200,000-300,000 premature deaths & $2 trillion lost productivity

$4.8
US government yearly budget
2020

$3.8
cost of destructive climate effects for USA
2020-2030

$0.02
US govt research into clean tech

TOTAL
$2.5
trillion

$.25
cost per year

$13.2
cost of destructive climate effects for USA
2030-2050

$10
net zero costs
2030-2050

$0.5 cost per year

$0.9
US military spending
2020

$5.1
US COVID bailouts, & emergency funding
2020

most zero carbon solutions are more expensive than fossil-fuel equivalents - that could change

carbon-free electricity, for example, would likely be about 15-20% more for public consumers

but fossil fuels only seem cheaper because the eco damage is not included in their price

Netzero Problems, Challenges, Responses, Solutions

COSTS

Who's going to pay for all this stuff?
Tax payers? Government? Corporates?

What about investment risk?
Lot of unknowns here

We need to start spending now, right?
The next ten years are essential

Where will the upfront cash come from?
A LOT is needed for infrastructure, etc.

**Climate crisis is already happening –
who will pay for the fallout?**

LOGISTICS

How are we going to build all this stuff?
Turbines, solar panels, transmission lines...

Grid expansion is a massive undertaking
Easier said than done!

PEOPLE

What about lost and displaced jobs?
Dramatic decrease in oil & gas = unemployment

**How to ensure individuals & communities
aren't disproportionately affected?**
Ensure material well-being for all

What about local opposition to disruptive

Raise lots of money to transition
Markets, industry & government together

Mix public & private funding
10% taxpayer, 90% market capital

Start spending now
The amount needed is less than coronavirus spend

Invest early in critical infrastructure
One of the biggest in history

Demo prototypes & de-risk new tech
Funded initially by government to reduce risk

Factor costs of mitigating climate effects
Floods, heatwaves, crop failure, migration

Understand this is a huge project
Perhaps the biggest in history

Come together to do this as a society
Public, markets, government & companies together

Support communities impacted by transition
Lower-income areas will likely suffer more

Create public acceptance of the possibilities
Public demand for clean energy will help

Generate new jobs
Netzero will actually create more opportunities

Support transitioning workers

Have a clear goal of netzero
Then we all align to achieve it

Envision multiple pathways & scenarios
No one single route to Netzero – keep options open

Sustain political will to see it through
Public demand for clean energy will help

Enhance & streamline policies & processes
Many weren't designed with climate change in mind

Test & prototype policies & standards locally
Before implementing them nationwide

Prioritise improving efficiency
For immediate easy wins

Research & develop new tech innovations
Offer tax breaks for companies to fund breakthroughs

Implement direct subsidies for netzero tech
As we currently do for fossil fuels

Consider carbon capture across the board
Direct carbon capture at source to trap emissions

Gradually phase out old fossil-fuel tech
And adapt and modify the rest

Develop & support bio- & electrofuels
We'll still need to use some liquid fuels

Use less stuff
Reduce demand, reuse & recycle

WILL

How do we create and sustain public enthusiasm?
Unclear how the public will receive all this change

Regulatory barriers – state & federal – are massive impediment to swift transition
Outdated policies created before climate crisis

Won't fossil fuel companies resist this massive change?
They are going to be the losers, right?

TECH

What about planes & ships which are not easy to switch to batteries?
There are never going to be electric 747s

And essential but fossil-fuel-dependent industries like steel?
Ingrained processes use a lot of CO_2

Or cement?
You literally can't make it without CO_2

What will happen to all the redundant fossil-fuel technology and machinery?
Vehicles, power plants, pipelines

Especially the massive & extensive petroleum & natural gas networks?
Including 4,000,0000 km of pipelines

HEY

Shouldn't we be reducing consumption?
Bring down our emissions and dispel the myth of continuous growth?

sources: Net Zero America (Princeton), New York Times, Rewiring America, Science Mag

Smoking Is Declining in Nearly Every Country

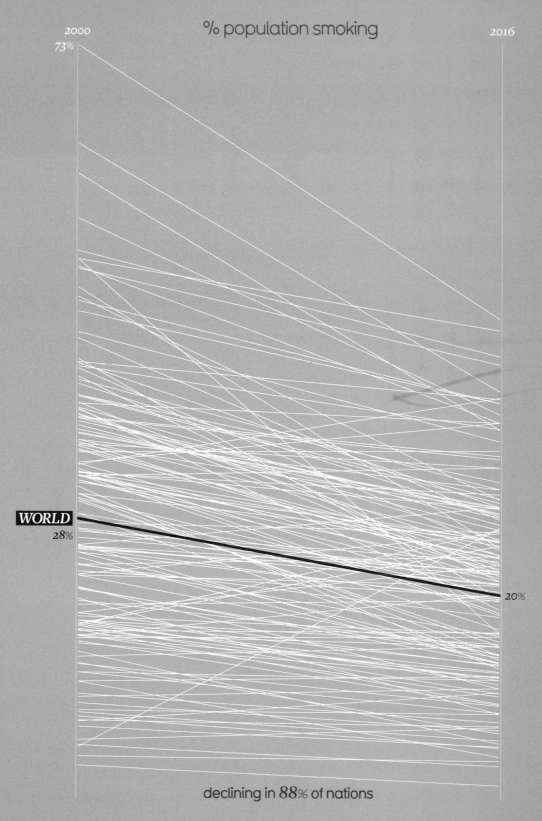

% population smoking

2000

2016

73%

WORLD
28%

20%

declining in 88% of nations

smoking-related deaths per 100,000

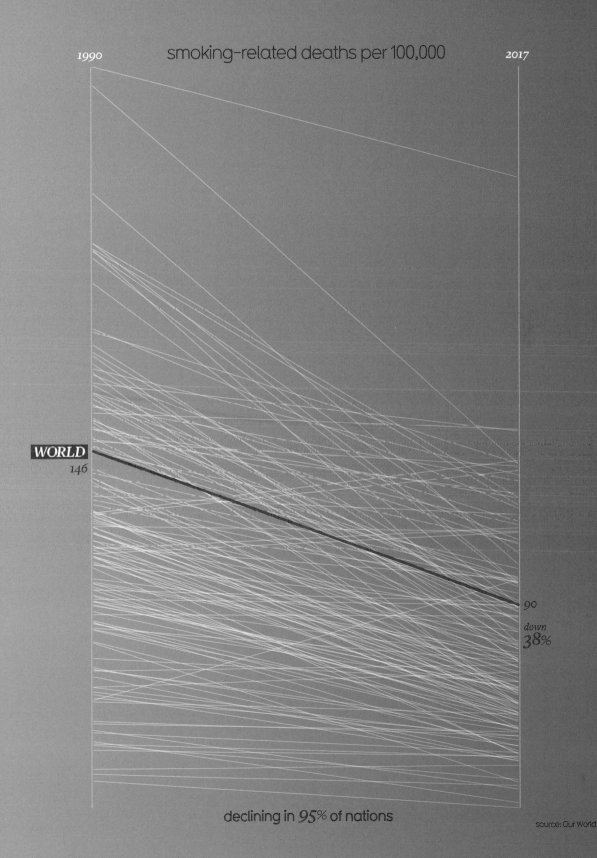

1990

2017

WORLD
146

90

down
38%

declining in *95%* of nations

source: Our World in Data

Some of the World's Poorest Nations Are Also The Most Generous

POOR & GENEROUS COUNTRIES

Myanmar ●

Indonesia ● Sri Lanka ●

Kenya ●

Liberia ● Gambia

Sierra Leone ● Nigeria ●

Uzbekistan ● Iran ●

Guatemala ●

Haiti ● Philippines ●

Malawi ● South Sudan ● Zambia ● Ghana ● Mongolia ●

Uganda ●

Tajikistan ● Honduras ● Jamaica ●

◄ ··

LOW WEALTH

Iraq ○

Afghanistan ○ Nepal ○ ○ Cameroon ○

○ ○

Tanzania ○ ○ Kosovo ○

Nicaragua ○

Mozambique ○ Pakistan ○ Algeria ○

Morocco

Ethiopia ○ ○

Burkina Faso ○○ ○ ○ ○○ ○○○

Niger ○ India ○ Egypt ○ Tunisia ○ Albania ○

○ Benin Cambodia ○ Armenia ○○

Madagascar ○ Rwanda ○

○ Palestine ○

POOR & LESS GENEROUS

○ Yemen

94 | 95

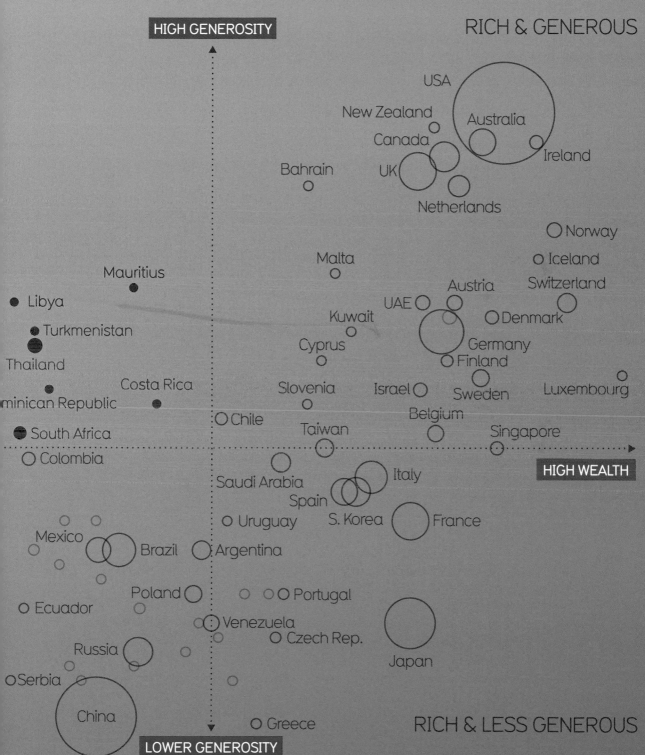

size of economy

HIGH GENEROSITY

RICH & GENEROUS

USA
New Zealand
Canada
Australia
Bahrain
UK
Ireland
Netherlands

Norway
Malta
Iceland
Mauritius
Switzerland
Libya
Austria
UAE
Denmark
Turkmenistan
Kuwait
Germany
Cyprus
Thailand
Finland
Costa Rica
Slovenia
Israel
Sweden
Luxembourg
minican Republic
Belgium
Chile
South Africa
Taiwan
Singapore
Colombia

HIGH WEALTH

Saudi Arabia
Italy
Spain
S. Korea
France
Mexico
Uruguay
Brazil
Argentina
Poland
Portugal
Ecuador
Venezuela
Czech Rep.
Russia
Japan
Serbia
China
Greece

RICH & LESS GENEROUS

LOWER GENEROSITY

source: Charities Aid Foundation, wealth per person
generosity measurd by helping strangers, donating money & volunteering time

We're Hacking Photosynthesis to Feed Our Growing Population

Improving the molecular efficiency of plants

UNMODIFIED

MODIFIED

up to **40%** larger

technology is being used on:

| soybean | rice | potato | tomato | aubergine |

and distributed free to small farms

source: Illinois University

A Natural Substance Could Replace Controversial Herbicide Roundup

Newly discovered sugar stops weed growth

7-deoxy-sedoheptulose

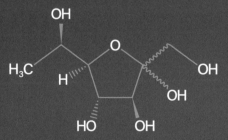

early tests show it's harmless to humans & animals

 Roundup (Glyphosate) is the most commonly used herbicide in the USA

 Discovered & brought to market by **Monsanto** (taken over by **Bayer** in 2018)

 Controversial due to evidence of **possible toxicity** in humans and animals

source: Nature Journal

Food Tech

Biofortified Cassava Is Set to Transform the Health of Millions

nearly **HALF A BILLION** Africans rely on cassava for **50%** of their calories

but cassava is

NUTRIENT **POOR** which contributes to → anaemia, diarrhoea deaths, cognitive problems

Hacking the genes

Biologists inserted two genes from thale cress... ...into cassava

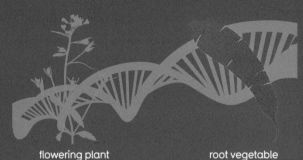

flowering plant   root vegetable

Transforming the nutrient profile

% of requirements of zinc and iron for women and young children

<10%

70%   50%

original cassava   biofortified

sources: American Council on Science and Health, Nature

Biofortified Golden Rice Could Reduce Lethal Vitamin A Deficiency

250m children worldwide suffer deficiency

375,000

187,000

cases of irreversible
childhood blindness

related
deaths

Golden rice can counter this

A staple food
bio-fortified

β
to contain high levels
of **beta-carotene**

which the body
turns into **Vitamin A**

levels per 50g

milk   spinach   golden rice   mango   carrots

| 75 | 230 | | 600 | 700 | 920 |
micrograms

child's daily requirement   **adult**

Golden rice is being approved for consumption

CANADA

USA

AUSTRALIA

NEW ZEALAND

Soon
BANGLADESH

where
30,000 children
go blind each year

source: World Health Organization, US National Institute of Health
sources: World Health Organization, US National Institute of Health

Rice Production is Improving, Boosting Food Security & World Health

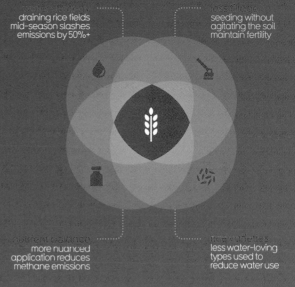

draining rice fields
mid-season slashes
emissions by 50%+

less tillage
seeding without
agitating the soil
maintain fertility

nutrient balance
more nuanced
application reduces
methane emissions

new varieties
less water-loving
types used to
reduce water use

Wider adoption could save 13.8 gigatonnes of CO2

0.4 million km²
current adoption

1.1 million km²
2050 goal

source: Project Drawdown

Rice Can Now Be Grown in Salty Water
Tonnes yielded per hectare

6.75
standard freshwater rice

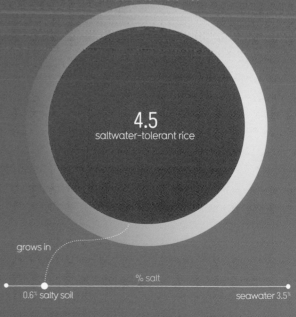

4.5
saltwater-tolerant rice

grows in

% salt

0.6% salty soil

seawater 3.5%

source: South China Morning Post

Canada has the largest protected boreal forest on the planet

boreal = high-latitude forests consisting mainly of conifers

created

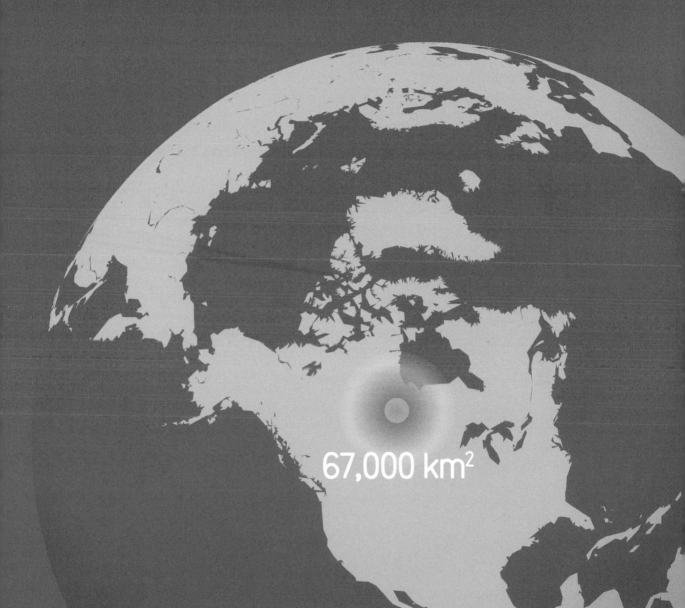

67,000 km²

source: BBC

The World Economy Has Ballooned
Trillion dollars

1968

2

$700
per person

2019

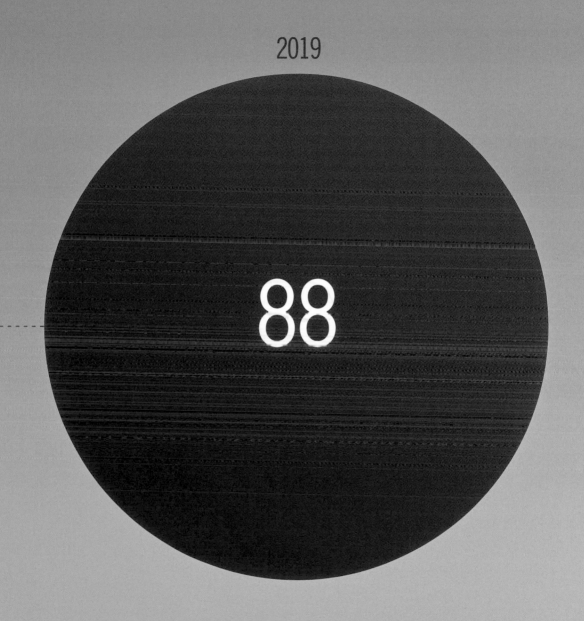

88

$11,400
per person

source: World Bank

The Potential of Geothermal Power Is Amazing

63,300,000 daily megawatt hours
Humanity's entire electricity usage

48,800,000
Global geothermal
energy potential

0.4

% we're currently using

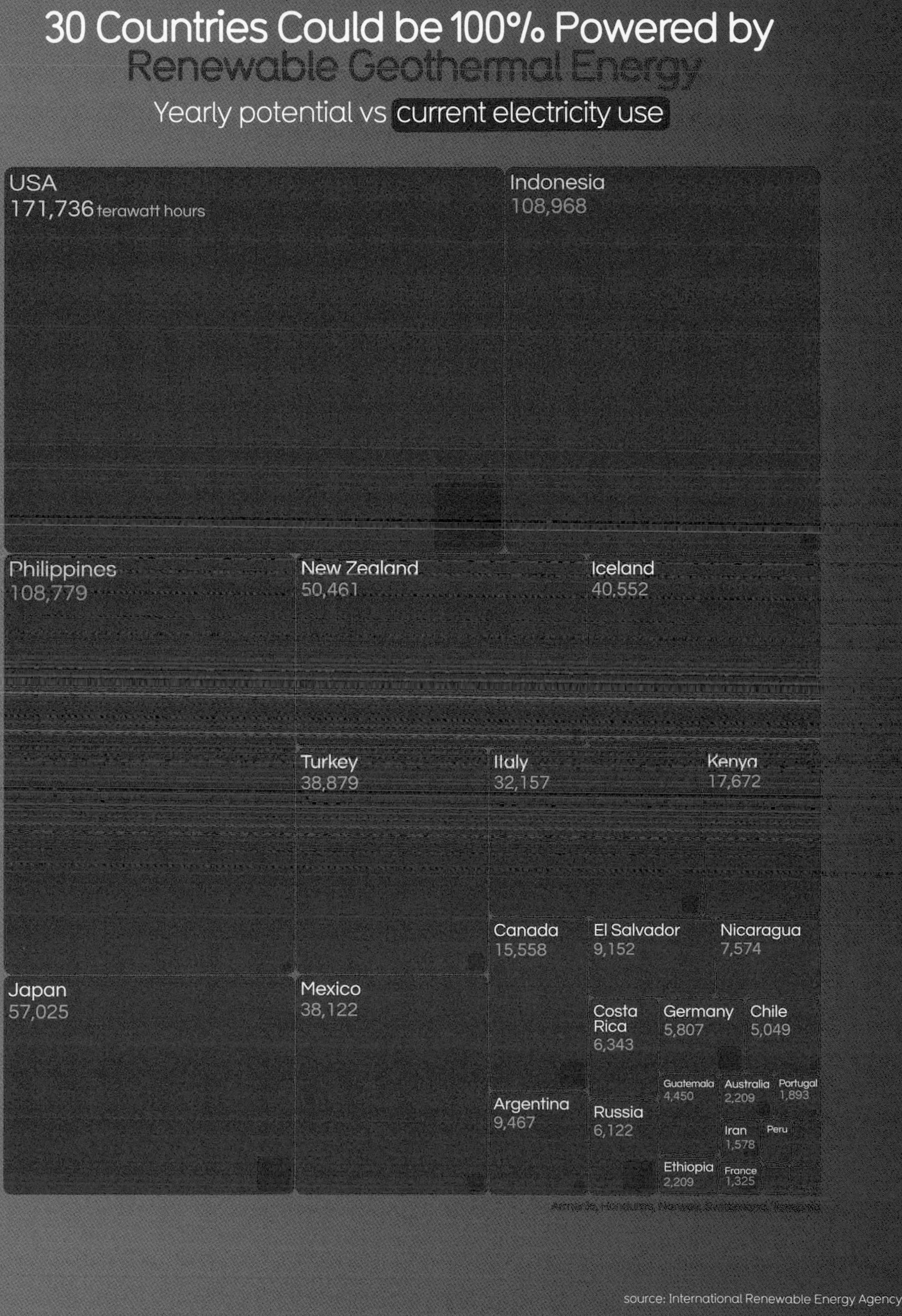

30 Countries Could be 100% Powered by
Renewable Geothermal Energy
Yearly potential vs current electricity use

USA
171,736 terawatt hours

Indonesia
108,968

Philippines
108,779

New Zealand
50,461

Iceland
40,552

Turkey
38,879

Italy
32,157

Kenya
17,672

Canada
15,558

El Salvador
9,152

Nicaragua
7,574

Japan
57,025

Mexico
38,122

Costa Rica
6,343

Germany
5,807

Chile
5,049

Guatemala
4,450

Australia
2,209

Portugal
1,893

Argentina
9,467

Russia
6,122

Iran
1,578

Peru

Ethiopia
2,209

France
1,325

Armenia, Honduras, Norway, Switzerland, Tanzania

source: International Renewable Energy Agency

Yay Africa!

The new African Union passport allows visa-free travel between 55 countries

source: Washington Post

When Submarine Internet Cables Arrived in Africa...

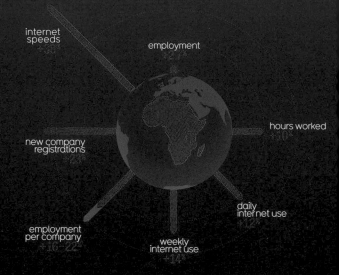

internet speeds

employment

hours worked
+10%

new company registrations

daily internet use
+12%

employment per company
+16-22%

weekly internet use
+14%

source: American Economic Review

Female Genital Mutilation Is Declining Across Most of the Continent
Prevalence by region %

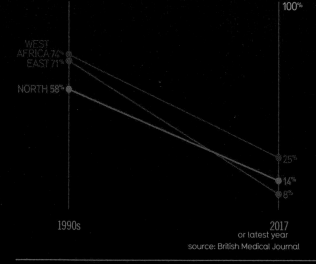

100%

WEST AFRICA 74%
EAST 71%

NORTH 58%

25%
14%
8%

1990s

2017
or latest year

source: British Medical Journal

South Africa Is Cutting HIV Infections
Despite suffering the world's biggest epidemic

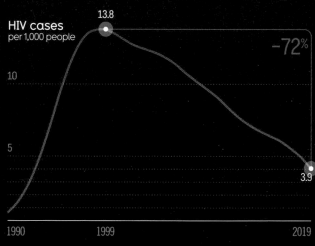

HIV cases
per 1,000 people

13.8

-72%

10

5

3.9

1990   1999   2019

sources: UNAIDS, Avert.org

Drones Have Revolutionised Medical Deliveries in Rwanda

DELIVERY TIME

30m vs 4h

with drone   pre-drone

CURRENT USAGE

35%

of blood supply delivered

MAX LOAD

1.75KG

3 units of blood

CRUISE SPEED

100km/h

in ideal conditions

African Countries Have Agreed to a New Free-Trade Bloc

 = total GDP

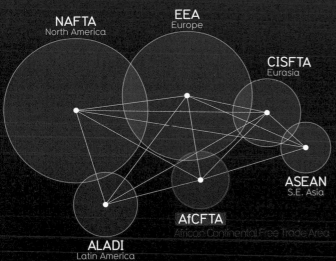

NAFTA
North America

EEA
Europe

CISFTA
Eurasia

ASEAN
S.E. Asia

AfCFTA
African Continental Free Trade Area

ALADI
Latin America

source: United Nations

Africa Leads the World in Mobile Money Transactions

Africa
396 million
Registered accounts

Rest of the World
470 million

source: Our World in Data, Africa = Sub-Saharan Africa

United Africa Is an Economic Powerhouse
Yearly GDP $US Tillions

Country	GDP
USA	21.4
China	14.3
Japan	5.1
Germany	3.9
India	2.9
UK	2.9
France	2.7
Africa	2.5
Italy	2.0
Brazil	1.8
Canada	1.7
Russia	1.7
S. Korea	1.6
Australia	1.4
Spain	1.4
Mexico	1.3

BILLIONS

Nigeria $448	Egypt $303	Algeria $171
	Morocco $120	Angola $88.8 · Ghana $67 · Tanzania $63.2
S. Africa $351	Ethiopia $95.9	Côte d'Ivoire $58.5
		Libya $52.1
	Kenya $95.5	Dem. Rep. Congo $50.4

sources:

COVERED AREA

Kigali
85km

from distribution centre

EFFECTIVE RANGE

22,500km²
covered area

source: Guardian

Access to Electricity Is Rising Across The Continent

% with power   1%   100%

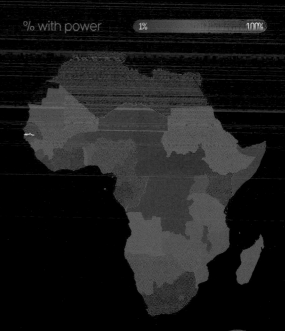

millions gaining
electricity per year

 9 ---- 20

2013   2019

source: International Energy Agency

The EU Is Leading on Recycling & Emissions

Its Economy Is Growing While Emissions Are Falling

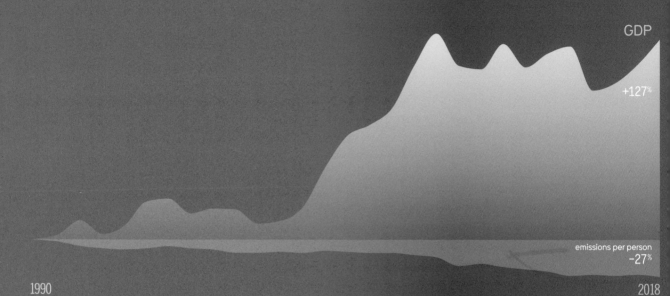

GDP

+127%

emissions per person
−27%

1990

2018

It Could Power the Entire World with Wind

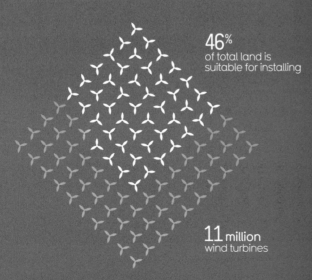

46%
of total land is
suitable for installing

11 million
wind turbines

Will Increase Its Offshore Wind Capacity by 250%

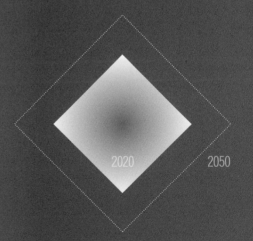

2020

2050

expected global demand 2050

EU wind energy generating potential

Paper Recycling Has Doubled over the Last 25 Years

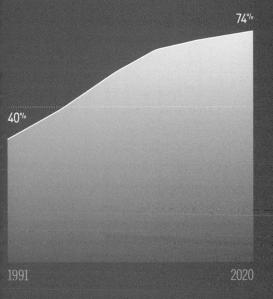

74%

40%

1991   2020

Some European States Are Recovering Almost All Plastic Packaging
Making it into new industrial products*

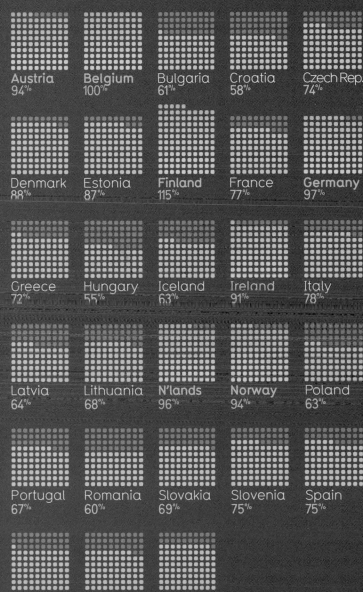

Austria 94%	Belgium 100%	Bulgaria 61%	Croatia 58%	Czech Rep. 74%
Denmark 88%	Estonia 87%	Finland 115%	France 77%	Germany 97%
Greece 72%	Hungary 55%	Iceland 63%	Ireland 91%	Italy 78%
Latvia 64%	Lithuania 68%	N'lands 96%	Norway 94%	Poland 63%
Portugal 67%	Romania 60%	Slovakia 69%	Slovenia 75%	Spain 75%
Sweden 71%	UK 68%	EU (average) 79%		

* wall insulation, slurry, lubricants, etc.

The EU has required all key electronic appliances to be *easier to repair*

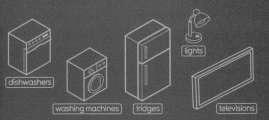

dishwashers — washing machines — fridges — lights — televisions

430 exajoules

497

sources: Independent, Energy Policy Journal, European Paper Recycling Council, Eurostat

62 Nations Have Corporal Punishment
In all settings: home, schools & prisons

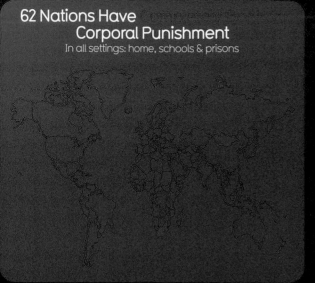

Corporal punishment = intended to cause physical pain   source: World Bank

Air Travel Has Never Been Safer
Millions of flights vs no. of fatal crashes

35

39

25   23

16   12   18   24

10

3

7

0

1993   zero fatal crashes! >>> 2017   2020

sources: Aviation-Safety.net, World Bank, commercial passenger crashes only

Atmospheric Acidity Is Back to Normal

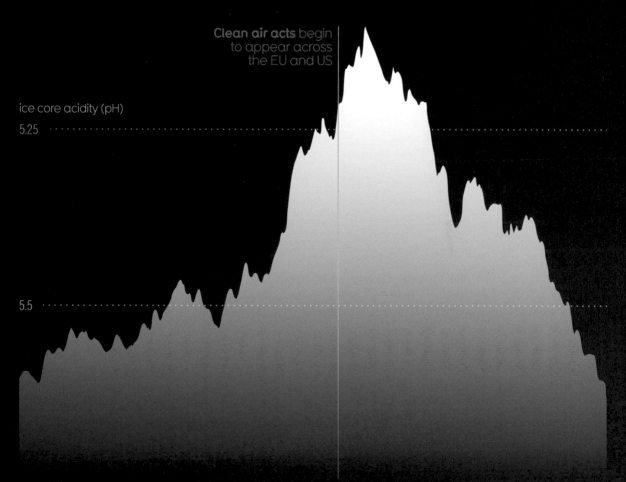

Clean air acts begin
to appear across
the EU and US

ice core acidity (pH)

5.25

5.5

1930   1970   2004

source: Kjær, Helle Astrid et al (2016), global

A New Device Uses Ocean Forces To Clean Plastic From Our Seas
From giant objects to microplastics

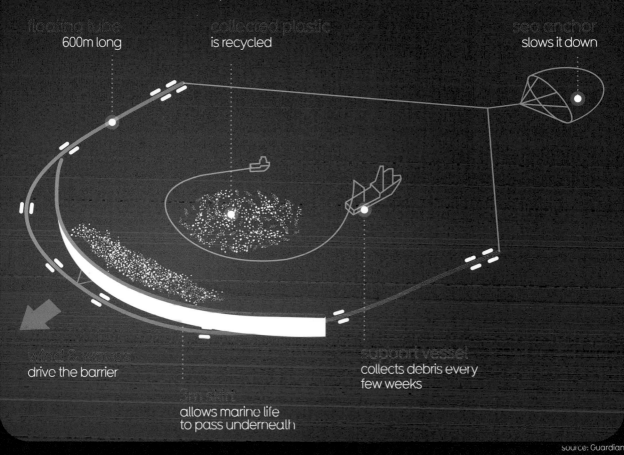

floating tube
600m long

collected plastic
is recycled

sea anchor
slows it down

wind & waves
drive the barrier

3m skirt
allows marine life
to pass underneath

support vessel
collects debris every
few weeks

source: Guardian

Russia's Child Mortality Is Down, Life Expectancy Is Up

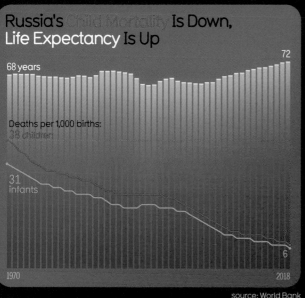

68 years

72

Deaths per 1,000 births:
38 children

31 infants

6

1970

2018

source: World Bank

Sweden Sends Almost No Trash to Landfill

Household waste
5 million tonnes

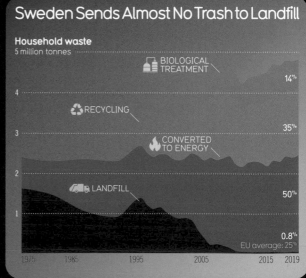

BIOLOGICAL TREATMENT
14%

RECYCLING
35%

CONVERTED TO ENERGY
50%

LANDFILL
0.8%
EU average: 25%

4

3

2

1

1975   1985   1995   2005   2015   2019

source: Avfall Sverige

Money Spent on Disadvantaged Kids Is a Great Long-Term Investment

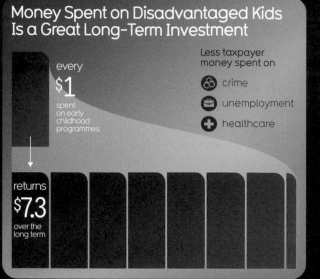

every
$1
spent on early childhood programmes

returns
$7.3
over the long term

Less taxpayer money spent on
- crime
- unemployment
- healthcare

source: University of Chicago

75% of All the Aluminium Ever Used in the USA Has Been Recycled

60 days
for a can to be recycled & back in use

98% BR
73% JP
Brazil & Japan are top recyclers of drink cans

only 9% of all plastics are recycled

sources: Aluminium.org, The Verge, Reuters

45,000+ Microgrids Are Out There
Small, affordable, hyper-efficient power grids essential bridge to a fossil-fuel future

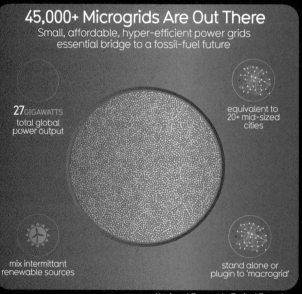

27 GIGAWATTS
total global power output

equivalent to 20+ mid-sized cities

mix intermittent renewable sources

stand alone or plugin to 'macrogrid'

source: Navigant Research, Project Drawdown

Most of the World Can Now Afford Mobile Internet
152 countries meet the affordability threshold*

better access to
banking & microfinance

health services

92%
OF GLOBAL POPULATION

education & books

public services

* 1 gigabyte of data for no more than 2% of average monthly income

source: World Bank

Finland Has Almost Eradicated Vaping

The government introduced pioneering e-cigarette regulations

 bans on flavours

 18+ age limits for buyers

 prohibition of marketing

 import restrictions

 banned in non-smoking areas

As a result, the country enjoyed drops in traditional smoking, without an accompanying rise in vaping

Finns smoking daily

25% (1998)   14% (2018)

Finns vaping daily
1%
Sweden* 4.4%
UK* 5.7%

*estimated
source: World Health Organization

Smoking Bans Improve Health

Declines after introduction of public smoking laws

child admissions for nose / throat / chest infections	−3.5%
premature births	−3.8%
asthma-related hospital visits	−9.8%
hospitalisations for acute coronary events	−12.0%
heart attack related health costs	−14.8%
hospitalisation of children with lower respiratory tract infections	−18.5%

source: National Institute for Health Research

Dutch Prisons Are Closing
And being turned into housing for refugees

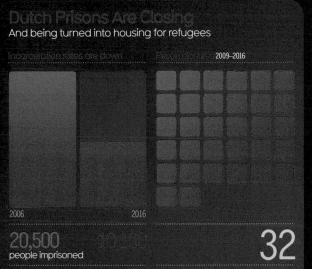

Incarceration rates are down   Prison closures 2009–2016

2006   2016

20,500
people imprisoned

32

sources: World Economic Forum, Fast Company

Most One-Year-Olds Are Vaccinated Against Three Lethal Diseases
Diphtheria, tetanus & whooping cough

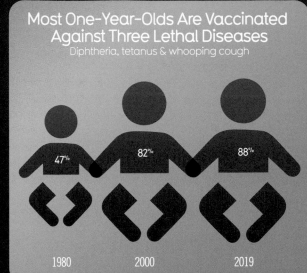

47%   82%   88%

1980   2000   2019

source: World Health Organization, global figures

World Vegetable Intake Almost Doubled
% increase in consumption per person

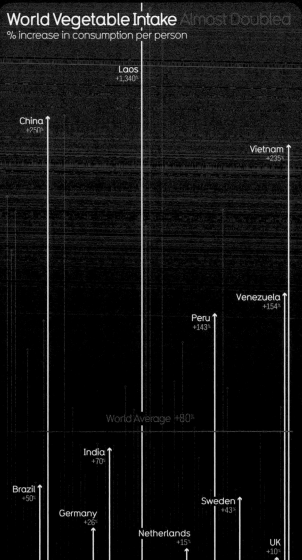

Laos +1,340%

China +250%

Vietnam +235%

Venezuela +154%

Peru +143%

World Average +80%

India +70%

Brazil +50%

Germany +26%

Netherlands +15%

Sweden +43%

UK +10%

% increase 1990-2013

source: Our World in Data

Cycling to Work Is on the Up
Cities with most bicycle commuters

Osaka 21%
The Hague 22%
Dresden 17%
Utrecht 34%
Eindhoven 24%
Bremen 19%
Amsterdam 40%
Malmö 25%
Beijing 32%
Copenhagen 30%
Aarhus 27%
Shanghai 20%

sources: Urban Audit, LTA Academy, June Jacobs Japan

More Afghan Girls Are Being Educated
Primary school enrolment rates

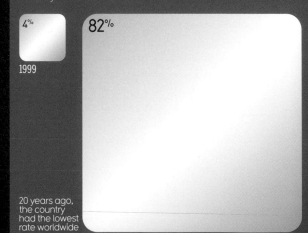

4%
1999

82%

20 years ago,
the country
had the lowest
rate worldwide

2018

source: UNESCO

Major Fashion Brands Are Going Fur-Free

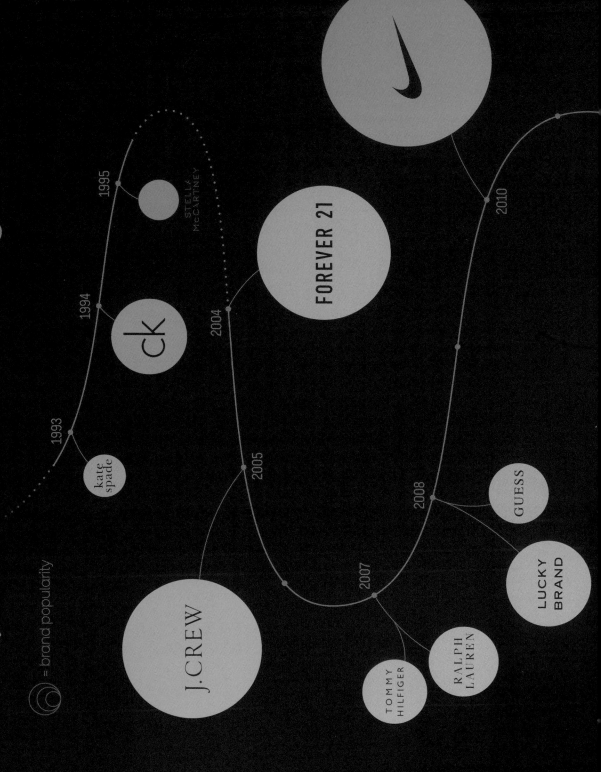

◎ = brand popularity

1993   1994   1995

kate
spade

ck

STELLA
McCARTNEY

2004

FOREVER 21

2005

J.CREW

2007

2008

TOMMY
HILFIGER

RALPH
LAUREN

GUESS

LUCKY
BRAND

2010

EU Countries Are Gradually Banning Fur Farming

partial ban

sources: Guardian, Independent, Harper's Bazaar

190 Nations Have Signed the Paris Climate Agreement
With only a few holdouts

size = level of emissions	Afghanistan	Albania	Algeria	Andorra	Angola	Antigua and Barbuda	Argentina
Belarus	Belgium	Belize	Benin	Bhutan	Bolivia	Bosnia and Herzegovina	Botswana
Cameroon	Canada	China		Central African Republic	Chad	Chile
Cote d'Ivoire	Croatia				Cuba	Cyprus	Czech Republic
Eritrea	Estonia				Eswatini	Ethiopia	Fiji
Grenada	Guatemala	Guinea	Guinea-Bissau	Guyana	Haiti	Honduras	Hungary
Italy	Jamaica	Japan	Jordan	Kazakhstan	Kenya	Kiribati	Kosovo
Liberia	Libya	Liechtenstein	Lithuania	Luxembourg	Macedonia	Madagascar	Malawi
Micronesia	Moldova	Monaco	Mongolia	Montenegro	Morocco	Mozambique	Myanmar
Niue	North Korea	Norway	Oman	Pakistan	Palau	Palestine	Panama
Russia		Rwanda	Saint Kitts and Nevis	Saint Lucia	St Vincent and the Grenadines	Samoa	San Marino
		Slovenia	Solomon Islands	Somalia	South Africa	South Korea	South Sudan
Switzerland	Syria	Tanzania	Tajikistan	Thailand	Timor-Leste	Togo	Tonga
Uganda	UK	Uruguay	Uzbekistan	Vanuatu	Vatican City	Venezuela	Vietnam

signed & ratified   just signed   not signed or leaving

Armenia

Australia

Austria

Azerbaijan

Bahamas

Bahrain

Bangladesh

Barbados

Brazil

Brunei Darussalam

Bulgaria

Burkina Faso

Burundi

Cabo Verde

Cambodia

Colombia

Comoros

Congo

Congo (Dem. Rep.)

Cook Islands

Costa Rica

Denmark

Djibouti

Dominica

Dominican Republic

Ecuador

Egypt

El Salvador

Equatorial Guinea

Finland

France

Gabon

Gambia

Georgia

Germany

Ghana

Greece

Iceland

India

Indonesia

Iran

Iraq

Ireland

Israel

Kuwait

Kyrgyzstan

Laos

Latvia

Lebanon

Lesotho

Malaysia

Maldives

Mali

Malta

Marshall Islands

Mauritania

Mauritius

Mexico

Namibia

Nauru

Nepal

Netherlands

New Zealand

Nicaragua

Niger

Nigeria

Papua New Guinea

Paraguay

Peru

Philippines

Poland

Portugal

Qatar

Romania

São Tomé and Príncipe

Saudi Arabia

Senegal

Serbia

Seychelles

Sierra Leone

Singapore

Slovakia

Spain

USA

Sri Lanka

Sudan

Suriname

Sweden

Trinidad and Tobago

Tunisia

Turkey

Turkmenistan

Tuvalu

Yemen

Ukraine

United Arab Emirates

Zambia

Zimbabwe

source: United Nations

LEVEL 4
13%

LEVEL 3
45%

Global Health Expenditure per Person
Has Never Been Higher

$320
2000

+194%

$542
2008

$940
2016

LEVEL 2
38%

The % of Global Population Covered by Essential Health Services Is Growing

LEVEL 1 4%

Australia	**Iceland**	**New Zealand**	**Switzerland**
Belgium	**Israel**	**Norway**	**Thailand**
Brunei	**Italy**	**Portugal**	**UK**
Canada	**Japan**	Singapore	Uruguay
Cuba	Luxembourg	**South Korea**	USA
Denmark	**Malta**	**Spain**	
Germany	**Netherlands**	**Sweden**	

Algeria	**Cze. Republic**	**Latvia**	**Romania**
Argentina	Dom. Republic	Lebanon	**Russia**
Armenia	**Ecuador**	Libya	**Saudi Arabia**
Austria	Egypt	**Lithuania**	**Serbia**
Azerbaijan	El Salvador	**Malaysia**	Seychelles
Bahamas	Estonia	**Maldives**	Slovakia
Bahrain	Eswatini	**Mauritius**	Slovenia
Barbados	Fiji	**Mexico**	South Africa
Belarus	Finland	Moldova	**Sri Lanka**
Belize	**France**	**Mongolia**	St Lucia
Bhutan	**Georgia**	Montenegro	Suriname
Bolivia	Greece	Morocco	Syria
Bosnia	Grenada	Myanmar	Tajikistan
Botswana	**Guyana**	N. Macedonia	Tunisia
Brazil	Honduras	N. Korea	**Turkey**
Bulgaria	**Hungary**	Namibia	Turkmenistan
Cabo Verde	Iran	**Nicaragua**	UAE
Cambodia	Iraq	**Oman**	Ukraine
Chile	Ireland	**Panama**	Uzbekistan
China	Jamaica	Paraguay	Venezuela
Colombia	Jordan	Peru	Vietnam
Costa Rica	Kazakhstan	**Philippines**	
Croatia	Kuwait	**Poland**	
Cyprus	Kyrgyzstan	Qatar	

Albania	Gambia	Mauritania	Timor-Leste
Angola	Ghana	Micronesia	Togo
Bangladesh	Guatemala	Mozambique	Tonga
Benin	Guinea-Bissau	Nepal	Uganda
Burkina Faso	Haiti	Nigeria	Vanuatu
Burundi	India	Pakistan	Yemen
Cameroon	**Indonesia**	Papua NG	Zambia
Côte d'Ivoire	Kenya	Rwanda	Zimbabwe
Djibouti	Kiribati	**Samoa**	
DR Congo	Laos	Senegal	
Equ. Guinea	**Lesotho**	Sudan	
Gabon	Malawi	Tanzania	

based on indicators like level of antenatal care, immunisation, TB & HIV treatments, cancer screening, hospital access, access to essential medicines

bold countries = free healthcare

source: World Health Organization

Unendangered Animals

= % change in population

	EXTINCT IN THE WILD	CRITICALLY ENDANGERED
Arabian Oryx		
Asian Crested Ibis		
Black Rhino		+135%
Blue Iguana		
California Condor		+3,400%
California Sea Otter		
Echo Parakeet		
Fin Whale		
Forest Owlet		
Giant Panda		
Green Sea Turtle (Florida)		
Guam Rail		+19%
Humpback Whale (South Atlantic)		
Iberian Lynx		
Indian Rhino (Kaziranga Park)		
Island Grey Fox		
Jaguar (Mexico)		
Lear's Macaw		
Mauritius Fody		
Mauritius Kestrel		
Mountain Gorilla		
North Island Kokako		
Northern Bald Ibis		
Okarito Kiwi		
Pink Pigeon		
Przewalski's Horse		
Rodrigues Fruit Bat		
Siberian/Amur Tiger		
Snow Leopard		
Southern White Rhino		
Steller Sea Lion		
W. Indian Manatee (Florida)		
Whooping Crane		

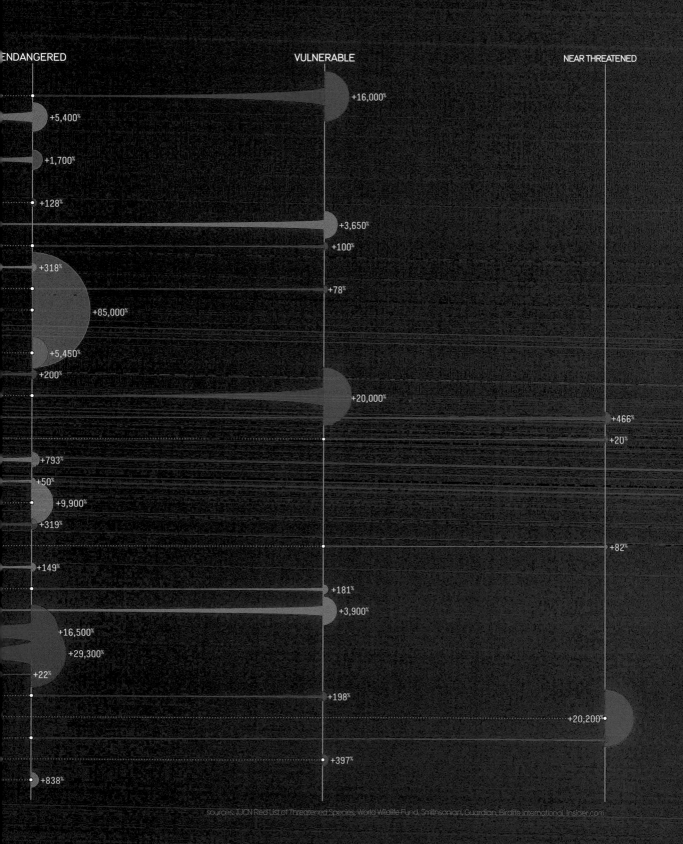

mammal   reptile   bird

ENDANGERED   VULNERABLE   NEAR THREATENED

+16,000%

+5,400%

+1,700%

+128%

+3,650%

+100%

+318%

+78%

+85,000%

+5,450%

+200%

+20,000%

+466%

+20%

+793%

+50%

+9,900%

+319%

+82%

+149%

+181%

+3,900%

+16,500%

+29,300%

+22%

+198%

+20,200%

+397%

+838%

sources: IUCN Red List of Threatened Species, World Wildlife Fund, Smithsonian, Guardian, Birdlife International, Insider.com

The Potential of Solar Is Amazing

63,300,000
daily megawatt hours
humanity's entire
electricity use

401,850,000
global solar energy potential

amount we're
currently using

0.5%

source: Sandia National Laboratories

Every Single Year We're Adding More and More
Worldwide solar capacity (gigawatts)

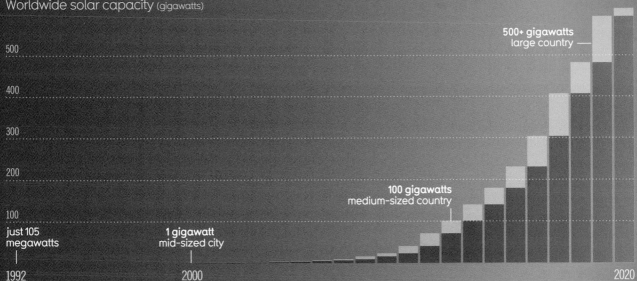

500+ gigawatts
large country

100 gigawatts
medium-sized country

just 105
megawatts

1 gigawatt
mid-sized city

1992   2000   2020

A gigawatt of solar supports about 2 million average African people, or 225,000 Europeans
source: International Energy Agency

Efficiency of Solar Panels Is Increasing
Major leaps

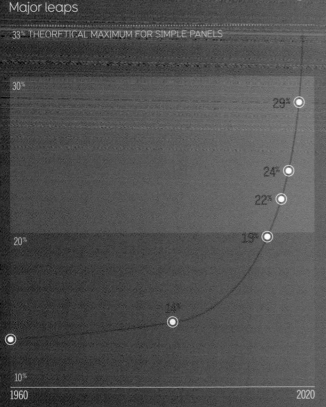

33% THEORETICAL MAXIMUM FOR SIMPLE PANELS

30%

29%

24%

22%

20%   19%

14%

10%

1960   2020

source: EnergySage

The Price Has Crashed
It's never been more competitive

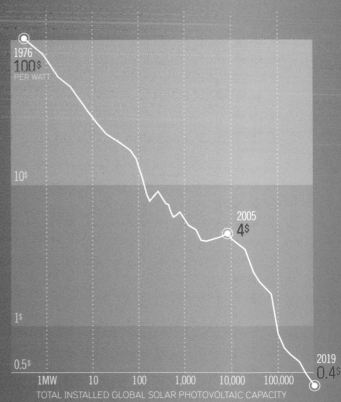

1976
100$
PER WATT

10$

2005
4$

1$

0.5$

2019
0.4$

1MW   10   100   1,000   10,000   100,000

TOTAL INSTALLED GLOBAL SOLAR PHOTOVOLTAIC CAPACITY

source: Our World in Data

Ukraine's first solar power plant has opened at the site of the Chernobyl nuclear disaster

source: Independent

Oil Fields Make Great Solar Farms
Just sayin'

the world's largest oil field is in Saudi Arabia

8,400 square kilometres

it's the size of Tokoyo, the world's largest city

CURRENTLY GENERATES **0.9**

petawatt hours of energy per year (1.4% of global use)

WOULD GENERATE **1.6**

petawatt hours as a solar farm (2.4% of global use)

source: Carbon Brief

Types of Solar Power

photovoltaic
solar panels convert energy from the sun into electricity

passive
floors, walls & windows of buildings designed to maximise & store solar energy

thermal
Arrays of many mirrors concentrate the sunlight onto a heatable fluid

concentrated
thousands of mirrors or lenses focus light onto a receiver which drives a turbine

India's PV Capacity Has Quadrupled
Gigawatts

+44%

36 2019 enough for 87 million Indian people

+39%

25 2018

+100%

18 2017

+400%

9 GW 2016

sources: IEA, Quartz

Spain Leads the World in CSP
Megawatts per km²

Spain 415

United Arab Emirates 121

Morocco 119

South Africa 33

Israel 29

USA 18

India 7

others 7

source: Statista.com

It's Legal to Be Homosexual in the Majority of the World's Countries

Egypt
Iran
Spain
Indonesia
Brazil
Ethiopia Bangladesh
UK
USA
France Turkey
Nigeria
Italy
Vietnam
China
India
Mexico Russia
Pakistan
Japan
Germany

population

source: International Lesbian, Gay, Bisexual, Trans and Intersex Association

300+ US Hospitals Created Their Own Non-Profit Drug Company

Providing generic drugs to hospitals at affordable prices to counter big pharma price hikes

Major price hikes in common drugs
since 2012

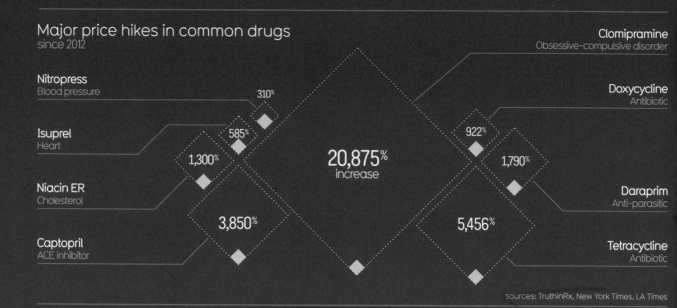

Nitropress
Blood pressure — 310%

Isuprel
Heart — 585%

Niacin ER
Cholesterol — 1,300%

Captopril
ACE inhibitor — 3,850%

20,875%
increase

Clomipramine
Obsessive-compulsive disorder

Doxycycline
Antibiotic — 922%

Daraprim
Anti-parasitic — 1,790%

Tetracycline
Antibiotic — 5,456%

sources: TruthinRx, New York Times, LA Times

186 countries agreed on a law to reduce plastic waste

Consent will be required before sending contaminated & unrecyclable plastics to other countries

86 nations agreed to curb aviation emissions

sources: International Civil Aviation Organization

29 US States, Australia, the UK, Japan, South Korea, & the EU have all adopted a renewable portfolio standard
It requires electrical utilities to get a certain % of their electricity from renewables –
in a flexible, market-driven way

Amazing Agreements

A New Global Plan Aims to Cut Emissions from International Shipping

Ships are a major contributor to global greenhouse gas emissions

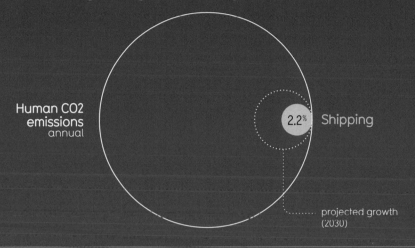

Human CO2 emissions
annual

2.2% Shipping

projected growth (2030)

The United Nations International Maritime Organization adopted a new plan to help solve the problem

CO2 emissions

−40%

−70%

2008   2030   2050

GHG emissions

−50%

2008   2050

energy efficiency
compulsory standards
for all international ships

sharing tech
to assist low-income
nations to transition

data collection
on fuel consumption
will be mandatory

source: United Nations International Maritime Organization

World's Biggest Tree-Planting Campaigns

India 116 million trees	Brazil 73	UK 50	27 Russia	Nepal Iceland
			30 Australia (Yarra Yarra)	20 Kenya
				20 Australia (Landcare)

Australia
1 BILLION
Forestry plan to meet the goal of the
Paris Climate Change Agreement by 2030

Pakistan
1 BILLION
Billion Tree Tsunami project spearheaded by
cricket-star-turned-politician Imran Khan

China
9.9 BILLION
largest in the world
Northeast Hebei & Qinghai provinces; Hunshandake Desert

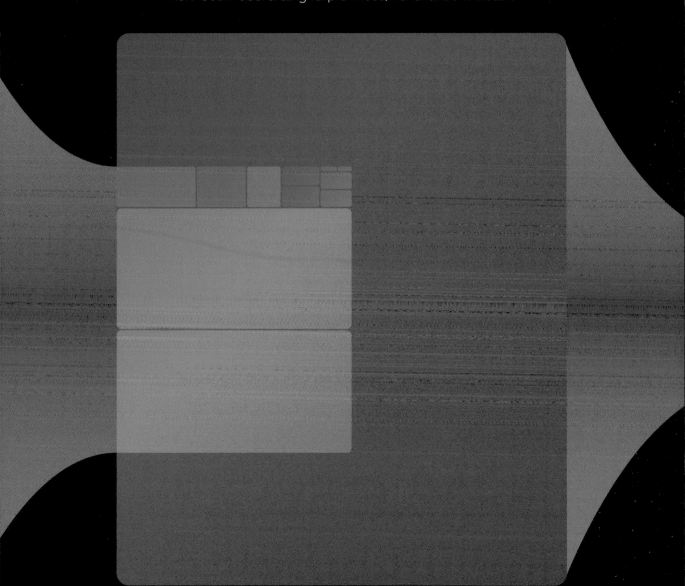

total trees that could realistically
be planted on Earth

1.2 TRILLION

1,200,000,000,000

Why Deforestation Is a Bad Idea
Because it...

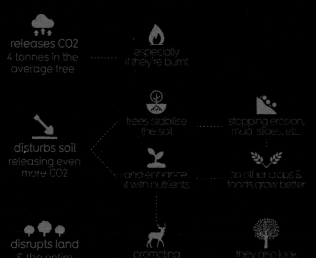

releases CO2
4 tonnes in the
average tree

especially
if they're burnt

trees stabilise
the soil

stopping erosion,
mud slides, etc.

disturbs soil
releasing even
more CO2

and enhance
it with nutrients

so other crops &
foods grow better

disrupts land
& the entire
ecosystem

promoting
diverse wildlife

they also look
beautiful!

Why Deforestation Happens
Different places, different reasons

INDONESIA & MALAYSIA
clearing for palm trees & oil

BRAZIL
cleared
pastures
for cattle

NIGERIA
massive charcoal
industry fuelled
by burning trees

LAOS
hardwood timber
industry (redwood,
teak, mahogany)

The World Is Ripe for Reforestation
Ideal regions for replanting

RULES FOR REFORESTATION

protect
existing
forests

plant on
degraded
land

engage
local
people first

'People cut down trees
not because they are
evil: they do it when
the incentives to cut
down trees are stronger
than the incentives
to leave them alone.'

BILL GATES

sources: World Economic Forum, EcoWatch, New York Times, BBC, Wikipedia, Bill Gates 'How to Avoid a Climate Disaster', Carbon Dioxide Removal Primer

More Places Are Protecting Animals

More Laws Are Coming into Effect

※ basic law against cruelty ⊗ civil code recognising sentient nature ☀ constitutional duty to protect animal dignity

Argentina	Australia	Austria	Azerbaijan	Bangladesh	Belgium	Brazil	Bulgaria
Canada	Chile	China	Colombia	Czech Rep.	Denmark	Dom. Republic	Egypt
Finland	France	Germany	Greece	Guatemala	Hong Kong	Hungary	India
Indonesia	Israel	Italy	Japan	Kazakhstan	Kenya	Lebanon	Malawi
Malaysia	Mexico	Myanmar	Nepal	Netherlands	New Zealand	Nicaragua	Nigeria
Norway	Pakistan	P. New Guinea	Paraguay	Peru	Philippines	Poland	Portugal
Romania	Russia	Serbia	Slovakia	Slovenia	S. Africa	S. Korea	Spain
Sri Lanka	Sweden	Switzerland	Taiwan	Tanzania	Thailand	Turkey	Uganda
Ukraine	UAE	UK	USA	Venezuela	Zambia	Zimbabwe	

sources: national Geographic, Global Animal Laws, Washington Post

Laws to Protect Animals & Pets Are Becoming More Widespread

US
acts of animal cruelty
now a federal crime

California
banned sale of non-rescue
animals in pet shops

Maine & Connecticut
abused animals can
now receive legal support

Maryland
third-party sales of
puppies & kittens banned

Ohio
animal cruelty upgraded
to a fifth-degree felony

Lebanon
introduced first
animal welfare law

UK
maximum jail sentences for
abusers now five years

England
banned all third-party
sales of puppies & kittens

Scotland
introduced stiffer penalties
for animal abuse

Taiwan
banned consumption
of cat & dog meat

China
banning raising cats
& dogs for meat

Shenzhen
banned consumption
of cat & dog meat

New Zealand
legally recognised as
'sentient' beings

protection of companion animals

low ● ● ● ● ● ● ● high

no data

sources: World Animal Protection, Guardian, BBC & others

Bans

Wild Animals in Circuses

Whale & Dolphin Captivity

Animal Testing for Cosmetics

● all animals ● some

● total ban ● ban on fish testing

Capturing Baby African Elephants for zoo's & Circuses Is Globally
BANNED

Elephants are intelligent
& social, and suffer when
removed from their herds

They can now only be
moved to African countries
with native elephants

Export overseas is
banned – except for
genuine conservation

And Some Animals Are Bouncing Back

Mountain Gorilla Numbers Rising
One of the most endangered species in the world

254	380	486	1,063
1981	2003	2010	2018

sources: Oryx, WWF, African Journal of Ecology

Giant Pandas Rebounding
Numbers in the wild **and** captivity

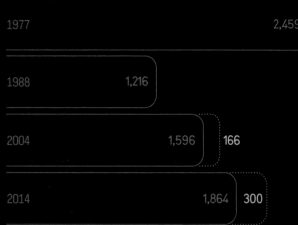

1977	2,459	
1988	1,216	
2004	1,596	166
2014	1,864	300

sources: World Wildlife Fund, IUCN Red List

Wild Tigers Increasing
Target: nearly doubling the population by 2022

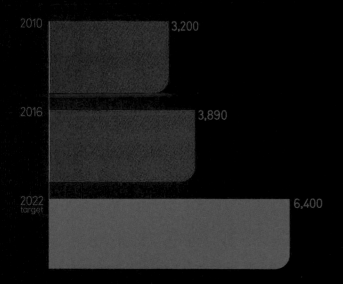

2010	3,200
2016	3,890
2022 target	6,400

source: World Wildlife Fund

Rhino Populations Growing
Thanks to law enforcement & population relocation

785 more rhinos

4,845 rhinos — 2012

5,630 — 2018

source: BBC Science Focus

Transport

Supercapacitor Buses Are a Thing Now
Shanghai has a network of efficient rechargeable buses

TRAVEL DISTANCE

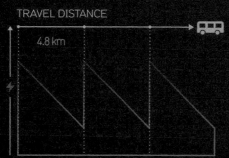

4.8 km

At each stop, the bus charges its capacitors enough to drive to the next one

The Inflatable Electric Scooter
The 'poimo' fits inside a backpack

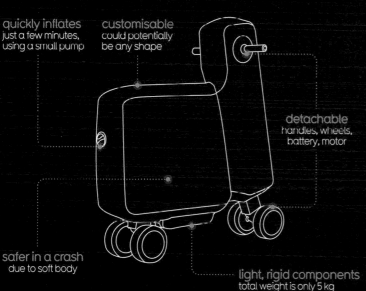

quickly inflates
just a few minutes, using a small pump

customisable
could potentially be any shape

detachable
handles, wheels, battery, motor

safer in a crash
due to soft body

light, rigid components
total weight is only 5 kg

Plastic Roads
Made from recycled waste

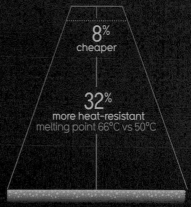

8% cheaper

32% more heat-resistant
melting point 66°C vs 50°C

Made of gravel, tar and a polymer glue extracted from plastic waste

1 km uses the equivalent of
1,000,000 plastic bags

3x longer lasting   **70%** faster to build   **4x** lighter

fully recyclable at end of lifespan

Currently made from polypropylene plastic found in

plastic furniture   plastic straws   cosmetic packaging   various car parts

bottle caps   plastic beer cups

Japanese Wooden Cars

A plant-based nanofibre makes them stronger than steel, but five times lighter, removing as much as two tonnes of carbon from the car's life cycle.

Hydrogen Shipping

shipping emissions
are high, around 2% of all greenhouse gases

green hydrogen
converted to ammonia fuel = zero emissions

▸000

sources: Shine.cn, PlasticRoad BV, Dezeen, Japanese Ministry of the Environment

Microscopic p[l]
algae in the u[p]
absorb four tir[...]
more CO2 than
the Amazon

as much as 40% of our emissions

the equivalent of 1.7 TRILLION trees

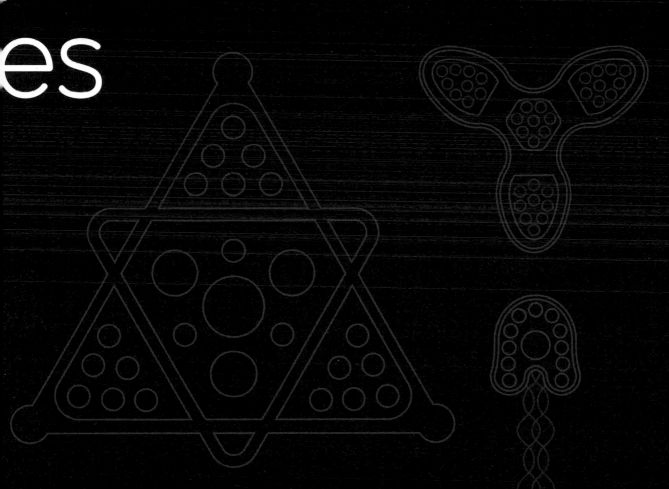

ytoplankton

per ocean

es

source: Buesseler et al (2020), BBC Science Focus Magazine

The Kigali Amendment is maybe one of the best global agreements you've never heard of

It seeks to eliminate the use of hydrofluorocarbons

HFCs are man-made gases

We use them to replace ozone-destroying CFCs

air conditioning

... used in ....

refrigeration

Unfortunately, they are also extremely potent greenhouse gases

HFCs up to 12,500x more

warming potential of CO2

They're emitted in very small quantities...

contribution to warming
2%

...but these quantities are rising

megatonnes emitted

2000   2010

Enter the Kigali Amendment

It aims to cut HFC use by 80–85% by the late 2040s starting...

2019

rich and developed economies
e.g. Canada & EU

2024

large & emerging economies
China & Brazil

2028

hot climate, lower-income nations
India, Pakistan, Saudi Arabia

118 countries have signed up so far

If successful, the Kigali Amendment will cut warming by 0.5°C by the end of the century

The Circular Economy Makes Sense

human-made materials synthesised, etc.

natural resources

composting

energy recovery turn into biofuels

waste*

recycle
re-insert materials
into the economy

design
long-lasting reusable
or recyclable products

PRODUCTION

production
using efficient &
renewable energy
& materials

reuse / repair / refurbish / re-manufacture

sorting
organised streams
& processes
to efficiently
& effectively direct
leftover materials

distribution
low-energy
packaging,
warehousing,
shipping,
delivery & retail

END OF LIFE

collection
avoid dumping
and waste

maintenance
right to repair,
replaceable parts,
long life

usage
sustainable
consumption
to increase
lifespan

END OF USE

USE

*managed landfill, minimal leakage, incineration with carbon capture

The Linear Economy

| PRODUCTION | USE | END OF LIFE | WASTE |

source: Ellen McArthur Foundation

Electric Cars Are a No-Brainer

They Are Inevitable
Million electric cars on the world's roads

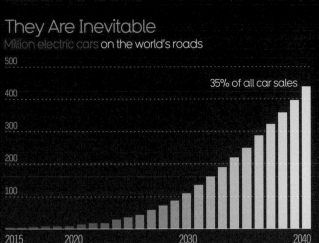

35% of all car sales

source: Bloomberg NEF

They Are Way More Efficient
% of energy delivered to wheels

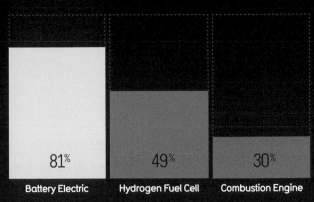

Battery Electric	Hydrogen Fuel Cell	Combustion Engine
81%	49%	30%

source: Princeton University

We Are So Close to the 'Tipping Point'
When different car types are most feasible....

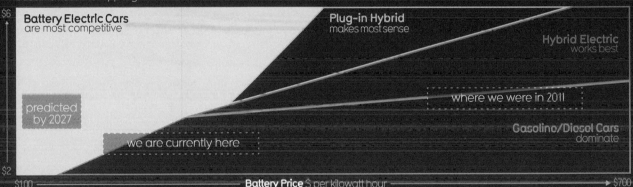

Gasoline Fuel Price $ per gallon

$6

Battery Electric Cars are most competitive

Plug-in Hybrid makes most sense

Hybrid Electric works best

predicted by 2027

where we were in 2011

we are currently here

Gasoline/Diesel Cars dominate

$2

$100 — **Battery Price** $ per kilowatt hour → $700

source: McKinsey

Norway Is Leading the Charge
Over half of new car sales are electric

NISSAN		8.5%
Volkswagen		7%
BMW		6%
TESLA		6%
MITSUBISHI		5%
VOLVO		3%
RENAULT		2%
HYUNDAI		1.5%
KIA		1.5%
others		9%

total **54.3%**

- extensive charging network 13,000+ points
- government subsidies on new cars
- reduced parking fees & road tolls

source: US Department of Energy

Along with California
electric vehicles sold

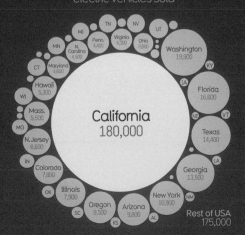

California 180,000

Washington 19,900
Florida 16,600
Texas 14,400
Georgia 13,500
New York 10,900
Arizona 9,800
Oregon 9,500
Illinois 7,900
Colorado 7,800
N. Jersey 6,600
Mass. 5,500
Hawaii 5,300
Maryland 4,600
N. Carolina 4,500
Virginia 4,300
Penn. 4,400
Ohio 3,800

MI TN NV UT MN CT WI MO IN OK SC KS AL KY IA NE VT LA NM

Rest of USA 175,000

source: US Department of Energy

...Europe and China
million sales 2018 2019 2020

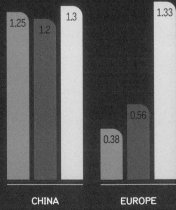

CHINA	EUROPE
1.25 1.2 1.3	0.38 0.56 1.33

source: BusinessWire

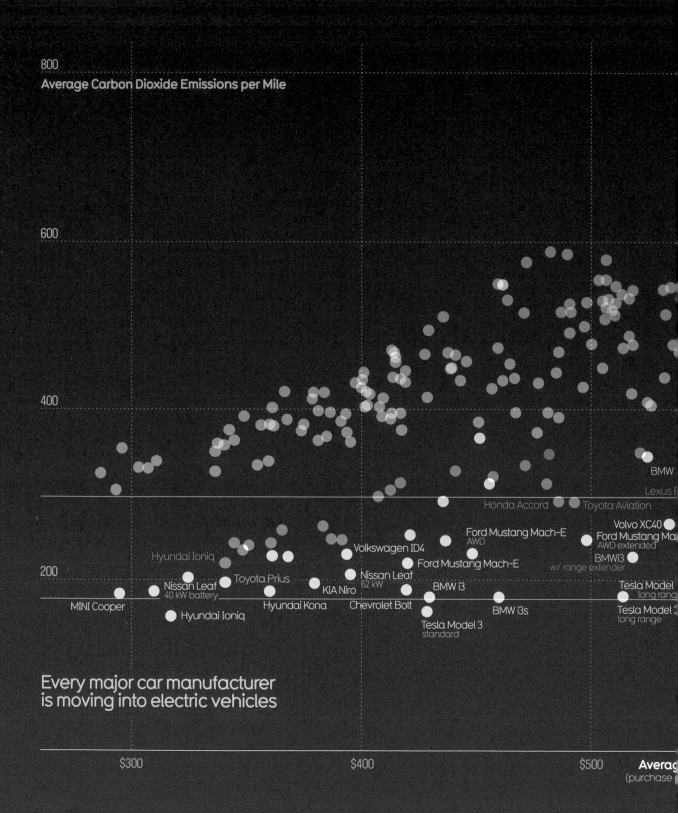

Average Carbon Dioxide Emissions per Mile

800

600

400

BMW

Lexus

Honda Accord   Toyota Aviation

Volvo XC40
Ford Mustang Mach-E   Ford Mustang Ma
AWD   AWD extended

Volkswagen ID4
BMWi3
Hyundai Ioniq   Ford Mustang Mach-E   w/ range extender

200   Toyota Prius   Tesla Model
Nissan Leaf   Nissan Leaf
40 kW battery   62 kW   long rang
          KIA Niro   BMW i3
MINI Cooper   Tesla Model 3
                Hyundai Kona   Chevrolet Bolt   BMW i3s   long range
        Hyundai Ioniq
                                        Tesla Model 3
                                        standard

Every major car manufacturer
is moving into electric vehicles

$300 $400 $500   Averag
                                                                                    (purchase

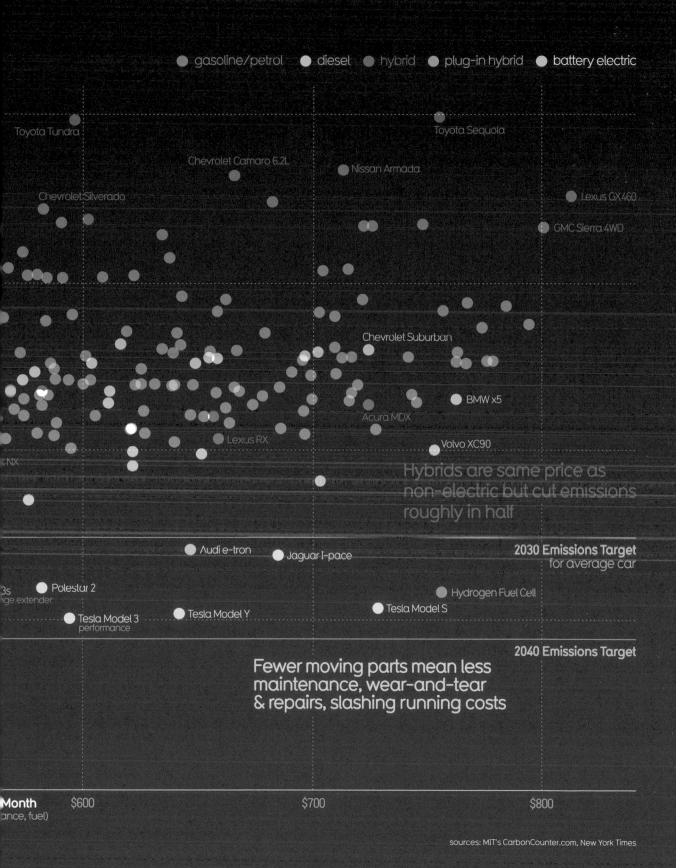

gasoline/petrol • diesel • hybrid • plug-in hybrid • **battery electric**

Toyota Tundra

Toyota Sequoia

Chevrolet Camaro 6.2L

Nissan Armada

Chevrolet Silverado

Lexus GX460

GMC Sierra 4WD

Chevrolet Suburban

BMW x5

Acura MDX

NX

Lexus RX

Volvo XC90

Hybrids are same price as
non-electric but cut emissions
roughly in half

Audi e-tron

Jaguar I-pace

2030 Emissions Target
for average car

3s
nge extender

Polestar 2

Hydrogen Fuel Cell

Tesla Model Y

Tesla Model S

Tesla Model 3
performance

2040 Emissions Target

Fewer moving parts mean less
maintenance, wear-and-tear
& repairs, slashing running costs

Month $600 $700 $800
ance, fuel)

sources: MIT's CarbonCounter.com, New York Times

Batteries Are Getting Better & Better

600*

2–3x
increase
likely

Rechargable Lithium-based Batteries Are the World Leader

very versatile
due to high weight-
to-power ratios

ideal for

phones

laptops

tools

electric cars

great cycle life
can be charged &
discharged many times

abundant material
enough world lithium for
one billion electric cars

They Are Getting Cheaper & More Powerful

Max. Energy Density
(watt hour per kilogram)

+600%   315

Cost
($ per kilowatt hour)

$1,000

210

$800

45

$350

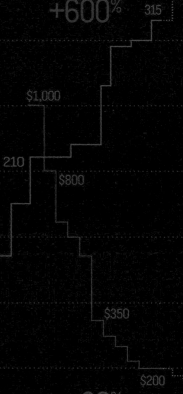

$200

−80%

$10

'Holy Grail' Price

| 1970 | 1980 | 1990 | 2000 | 2010 | 2020 | 2030 |

sources: Bloomberg NEF, Chen-Xi Zu et al (2011), * = theoretical limit for Liithium batteries is 1,000 Wh/Kg

Old-School, Current & Future Battery Technology

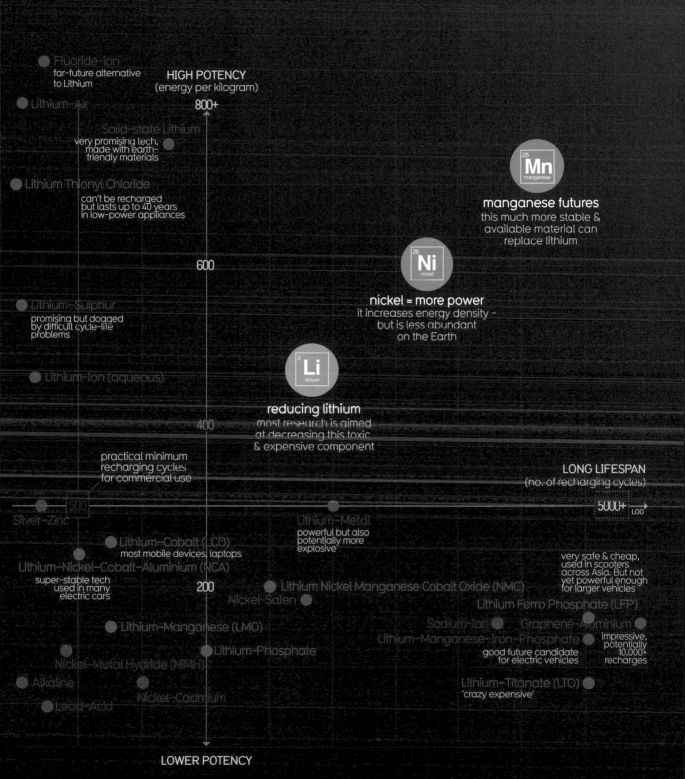

Fluoride-ion
far-future alternative
to Lithium

HIGH POTENCY
(energy per kilogram)

Lithium-Air

800+

Solid-state Lithium
very promising tech,
made with earth-
friendly materials

Lithium Thionyl Chloride
can't be recharged
but lasts up to 40 years
in low-power appliances

Mn
25
manganese

manganese futures
this much more stable &
available material can
replace lithium

600

Ni
28
nickel

Lithium-Sulphur
promising but dogged
by difficult cycle-life
problems

nickel = more power
it increases energy density -
but is less abundant
on the Earth

Lithium-Ion (aqueous)

Li
3
lithium

reducing lithium
most research is aimed
at decreasing this toxic
& expensive component

400

practical minimum
recharging cycles
for commercial use

LONG LIFESPAN
(no. of recharging cycles)

500

5000+ LOG

Silver-Zinc

Lithium-Metal
powerful but also
potentially more
explosive

very safe & cheap,
used in scooters
across Asia. But not
yet powerful enough
for larger vehicles

Lithium-Cobalt (LCO)
most mobile devices, laptops

Lithium-Nickel-Cobalt-Aluminium (NCA)
super-stable tech
used in many
electric cars

200

Lithium Nickel Manganese Cobalt Oxide (NMC)

Lithium Ferro Phosphate (LFP)

Nickel-Salen

Lithium-Manganese (LMO)

Sodium-ion

Graphene-Aluminium

Lithium-Manganese-Iron-Phosphate
good future candidate
for electric vehicles

impressive,
potentially
10,000+
recharges

Nickel-Metal Hydride (NiMH)

Lithium-Phosphate

Alkaline

Nickel-Cadmium

Lithium-Titanate (LTO)
'crazy expensive'

Lead-Acid

LOWER POTENCY

sources: Forbes, Associated Press, Battery University, Yang et al (2019), Broux (2018), Wikipedia

Fewer People Are Suffering from
Neglected Tropical Diseases

29% of world population affected

21%

2010   2017

Major NTDs

 = impact on lives (DALYS)

Leprosy
Curable bacterial
infection causes
skin & nerve
damage

Echinococcosis
A hookworm
disease, often
spread by dogs,
causing cysts

Trematodiasis
Liver and lung
disease carried
in fish and
vegetables

River blindness
Parasitic infection
with severe
itching & eventual
blindness

Leishmaniasis
Spread by sand
flies, triggering
skin sores and
organ damage

Yaws
Chronic infection
affecting the skin,
bone and
cartilage

Rabies
Fatal infection of
brain and nerves,
spread by dogs &
bats

Cysticercosis
Tapeworm
infection causes
cysts in eyes,
brain & spine

Lymphatic filariasis
Chronic disease
from microscopic
worms, spread by
mosquito bites

Dengue fever
Mosquito-borne
infection with
flu-like
symptoms

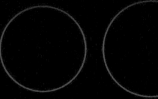

Schistosomiasis
Flatworm infection
causing organ
damage and
stunted growth

Helminthiasis
Parasitic worm
disease causing
gastrointestinal
symptoms

sources: United Nations, World Bank, World Health Organization

A Wall of Fertile Land Will Cross Africa
The Great Green Wall is a mosaic of trees, cropland & ecosystems

improve food & water supply

restore 1m km2 of degraded land

create 10 million rural jobs

sequester carbon dioxide

prevent migration out

PROGRESS
15%
completed

FINAL LENGTH
8,000 km

source: GreatGreenWall.org

carbon taxes/pricing

fees that must be paid when
greenhouse gasses are released
into the atmosphere

Current emitters don't pay for the
climate damage caused by emissions

That's why fossil fuels stay artifically
cheap to produce and use.
Their true cost is hidden.

(usually hundreds of billion dollars a year – hurricanes, wildfires, floods, heatwaves, forest fires)

Carbon pricing reinjects these costs
back into the economy to create a
true price for emissions.

This coaxes businesses to pay for
environmental pollution

so returning any revenue back to
taxpayers & society

If done well, carbon pricing can...

use market forces effectively to encourage change
act as a disincentive to emit greenhouse gases
spur creation of carbon-free alternatives
reduce consumption of carbon fuels
motivate improvement of energy efficiency
peed up the transition to zero-carbon fuels
reduce or even eliminate the use of fossil fuels
raise money to combat climate fallout & rising energy costs

It's challenging to make work, but currently the best option for a fair, global framework that will actually drive down emissions

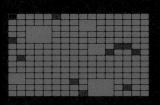

the Paris Agreement has many provisions for carbon pricing

33%
10 YEARS

52%
20 YEARS

models show carbon taxes & pricing substantially reducing emissions

many systems are already in place – or planned....

sources: Carbon Tax Center, National Geographic, Carbon Brief, Clean Technica, World Bank, New York Times

Carbon Pricing Is Catching On Around the World

57 schemes implemented or scheduled worldwide

$230 billion carbon trading global market already established

on track to become one of the biggest commodity markets

46 national, 28 subnational regions and cities

growing fast year on year ~ 30% in 2019

11 gigatonnes or 20% of human emissions covered

Global Carbon Schemes
IN OPERATION   SCHEDULED   UNDER CONSIDERATION

WASHINGTON
OREGON
MEXICO
COLOMBIA
BRAZIL
CHILE
ARGENTINA

BRITISH COLUMBIA 2008

REVENUE-NEUTRAL carbon tax on households & industries

Money generated fed tax rebates and tax reductions

Reduced emissions with no hurt to jobs or households

VERDICT SUCCESS

CALIFORNIA 2017

CAP & TRADE covers power plants, refineries & industry

Initial price was set too high, resulting in modest results

Emissions reduced but mostly due to other measures

VERDICT MIDDLING

What Should Carbon's Price Be?
Calculating the correct price for carbon pollution is difficult as the social cost varies between countries

CARBON PRICE $ PER TONNE OF CO2e $40 THE MINIMUM PRICE TO MEET PARIS CLIM

CALIFORNIA $16   UK $25   IRELAND $38   SPAIN & FRANCE   NORWAY & CANADA

types

🛢 **WELL HEAD** the company which extracts the carbon is taxed

💲 **REVENUE-NEUTRAL** softens impact of pricing by reducing taxes elsewhere in society

⇄ **CAP & TRADE** companies buy, sell & trade a fixed number of permits to emit carbon

⊛ **HYBRID** a mix, perhaps involving subsidies, feed-in tariffs, direct carbon taxes, etc.

ENGLAND   2013

CARBON PRICING was levied across the industry

Cost the average household £39 ($54) per year

Coal use declined massively 40% to 3%

VERDICT KINDA WORKED

CHINA   2021

National **CAP& TRADE** system planned after tests in cities

Gradual expansion to steel, concrete & electricity sectors

Aiming to learn from the EU & California's mistakes

VERDICT WE'LL SEE...

EUROPEAN UNION   2005

First in the world to launch a **CAP & TRADE** carbon scheme

Early phases failed – too many permits swamped the market

Later phases added sectors, tightened limits, worked better

But complex & technical set-up (typical EU!) caused problems

Phase 04 starting in 2021, with improvements to the system

Emissions have fallen 21% but other factors are at play

VERDICT HIT & MISS

COLOMBIA $84   CHILE $89   SWITZERLAND $96   SINGAPORE $101   JAPAN $106   MEXICO $109   SWEDEN $127   POLAND $129

sources: World Bank, New York Times

US Smoking Rates Are the Lowest Ever

45%
40%
15%

1944
2019

source: Gallup

Suicide Attempts Among LGBT Teens Fell After Same-Sex Marriage Was Legalised
% US LGBT students attempting to take their own life

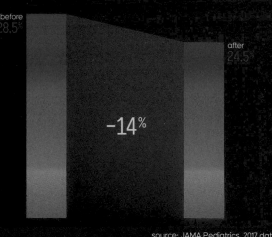

before
28.5%

after
24.5%

-14%

source: JAMA Pediatrics, 2017 data

Oil Spills Have Decreased
thousand tonnes spilt

636 Main spill:
Independenta (95)
Romanian carrier collided
with a Greek freighter at the
southern entrance of
Bosphorus, Turkey

431

383

384

ABT Summer (260)
Liberian flag, Iranian oil.
Sank due to unexplained
explosion 700 miles off the
coast of Angola

190

Sanchi (113) **116**
Iranian-owned tanker hit a
Hong Kong-flagged cargo ship
300 km off Shanghai, China

1970

2019

Norway Recycles Almost All of Their Plastic Bottles

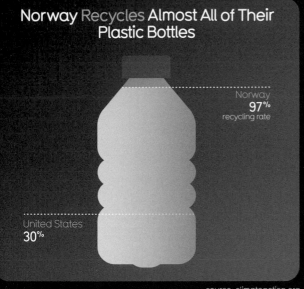

Norway
97%
recycling rate

United States
30%

source: climateaction.org

These Cities are Ruling Bike-Sharing
rental bikes per 100,000 people

Paris
97

Hangzhou
54

Nantes
40

Bordeaux
93

Antwerp
100

Helsinki
42

Tel Aviv
52

Oslo
46

Seville
39

source: COYA Bike Index 2019

Most Women Have Some Legal Access to Abortion
Reasons permitted:

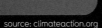

any	social/economic	life at risk only	health	none
36%	23%	22%	14%	5%

still prohibited in:
Angola • Congo • Dom. Rep • Egypt • El Salvador • Haiti • Honduras • Iraq • Jamaica • Laos • Madagascar • Mauritania • Nicaragua • Philippines • Senegal • Sierra Leone • Suriname

source: Center for Reproductive Rights

Soy & Oat Milk Are the Most Sustainable

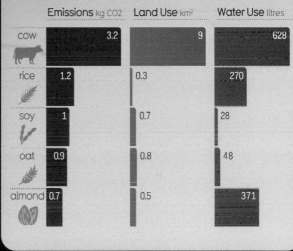

	Emissions kg CO2	Land Use km²	Water Use litres
cow	3.2	9	628
rice	1.2	0.3	270
soy	1	0.7	28
oat	0.9	0.8	48
almond	0.7	0.5	371

source: New York Times

Global Literacy Is Increasing

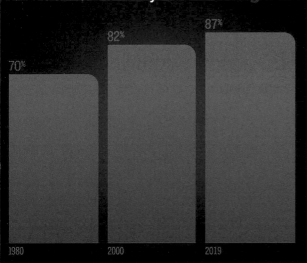

70%
82%
87%

1980
2000
2019

source: World Bank

Ecosia is a search engine that plants trees every time you search.

82,500,000 so far
One every 1.3 seconds

source: Ecosia

A 100% Biodegradable, Comfortable Sanitary Pad Has Finally Been Developed

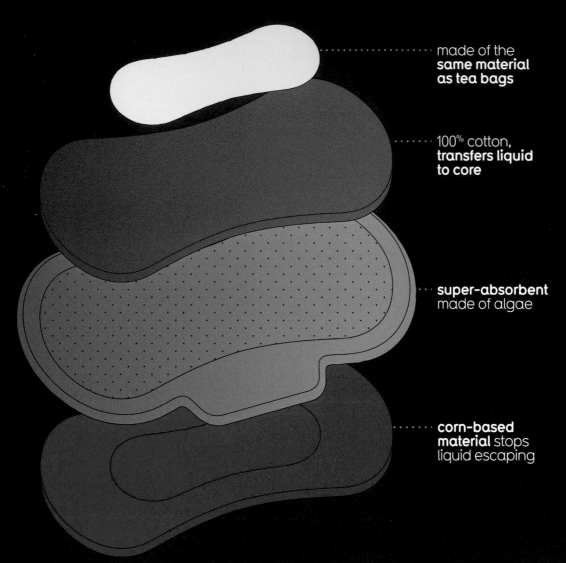

made of the **same material as tea bags**

100% cotton, **transfers liquid to core**

super-absorbent made of algae

corn-based material stops liquid escaping

the average pad is 90% plastic

tampon applicator, string & packet are also plastic

BIO PAD
1.5 to 6 months to degrade

Nearly a Quarter of the World Now Supports
Sales Tax-Free or Reduced-Cost Menstrual Products

Australia, Canada, Colombia, India, Ireland, Jamaica, Kenya, Lebanon
Malaysia, Maurilius, Nicaragua, Nigeria, Tanzania, Trinidad & Tobago

Alaska, Arizona, Colorado, Connecticut, D.C., Delaware, Florida, Illinois, Maryland, Massachusetts, Minnesota,
MontanaNebraska, Nevada, New Hampshire, New Jersey, New York, Ohio, Oregon, Pennsylvania, Wisconsin

**17 billion tampons
are sold yearly**

**and at least 40%
more sanitary pads**

**98% are discarded,
ending up in landfills**

**and take hundreds
of years to degrade**

NORMAL PAD
centuries to degrade

sources: University of Utah, Civio, BBC, Tax Foundation

Yay Germany!

Germany's Renewable Energies Are Pushing Back Fossil Fuels

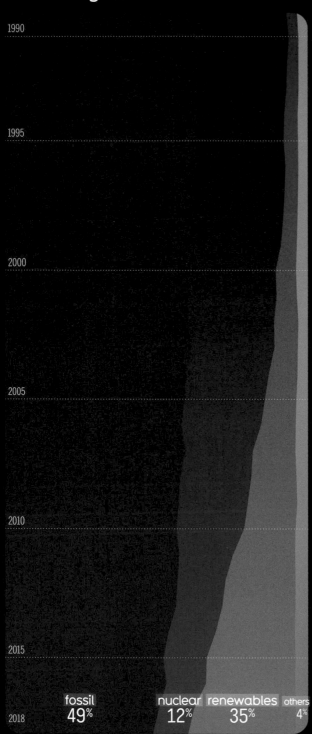

1990
1995
2000
2005
2010
2015
2018

fossil	nuclear	renewables	others
49%	12%	35%	4%

source: Energie AG

Over Two-Thirds of Refugees in Germany Are in Work after Five Years

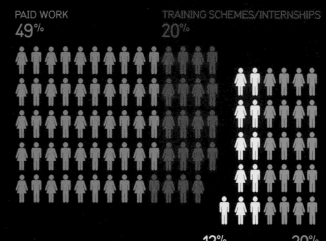

PAID WORK
49%

TRAINING SCHEMES/INTERNSHIPS
20%

12%
'MINI JOBS'
earning less than
€450 per month

20%
UNEMPLOYED

source: Deutsche Welle, Data 2013-2018

The first country in the world to ban chick-shredding

the chicken & egg industry's 'dirty secret'

all newborn
male chicks
are killed
at birth

often by just
being thrown
into mechanical
shredders

because they
can't lay eggs
so are not
profitable

45 MILLION CHICKS KILLED A YEAR IN GERMANY ALONE
123,000 per day   5,100 per hour   85 per minute

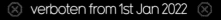

⊗ verboten from 1st Jan 2022 ⊗

farmers will use tech to determine
a chick's sex before birth

source: DW.com

More and More People Are Gaining
Access to Electricity

100% of world population

89.6%

71.5%
plugged in

340,000
people per day

New Ways to Create & Store Energy

In-Stream Hydro **Generates Zero-Carbon Power Without Environmental Damage**

Small hydropower units can be placed in rivers or even inside city water pipes

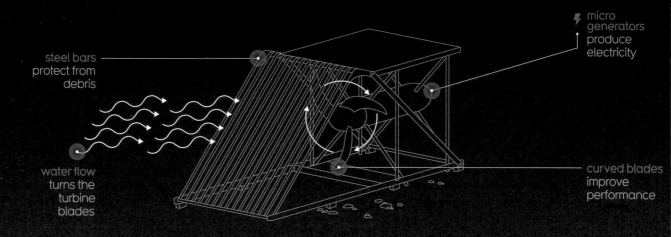

steel bars protect from debris

micro generators produce electricity

water flow turns the turbine blades

curved blades improve performance

From Alaska to Nepal, schemes are being proposed in remote communities to replace old, dirty and expensive diesel generators

PROS

 predictable power output

 easy to install and maintain

 very little space required

 low costs (no dams)

 low ecological impact

 minimal noise disturbance

CONS

 low power in summer months

 care to avoid hurting fish

source: Smart Hydro Power

Rivers Could Generate Thousands of Power Plants' Worth of Energy

Salt is made of charged particles, positive & negative

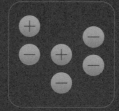

When salt water meets fresh water, the particles detach

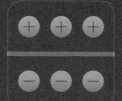

Newly invented blue membrane separates them

Separate areas are then connected by wire to generate electricity

source: Science Magazine

Coating Solar Panels with Carbon Nanotubes* Can Triple Efficiency

Combining Solar Panel Technologies Could Boost Energy Production by a Third

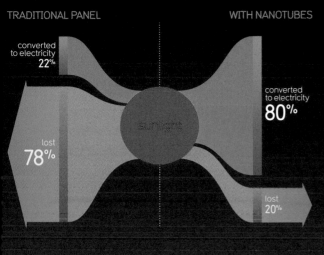

TRADITIONAL PANEL

WITH NANOTUBES

converted to electricity
22%

sunlight

lost
78%

converted to electricity
80%

lost
20%

* tubes one millionth of a millimetre wide with extraordinary electrical & thermal properties

source: Rice University

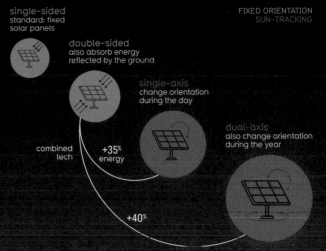

FIXED ORIENTATION   SUN-TRACKING

single-sided
standard: fixed solar panels

double-sided
also absorb energy reflected by the ground

single-axis
change orientation during the day

dual-axis
also change orientation during the year

combined tech

+35% energy

+40%

source: newscientist.com

A New Device Can Harness Electricity from Raindrops

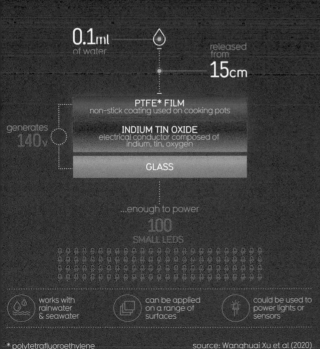

0.1ml
of water

released from
15cm

PTFE* FILM
non-stick coating used on cooking pots

INDIUM TIN OXIDE
electrical conductor composed of indium, tin, oxygen

GLASS

generates
140v

...enough to power
100
SMALL LEDS

works with rainwater & seawater

can be applied on a range of surfaces

could be used to power lights or sensors

* polytetrafluoroethylene

source: Wanghuai Xu et al (2020)

Ingenious Concrete-Filled Trains Act as Giant Batteries

Excess power slowly pulls trains up a slope

Regenerative braking produces electricity on the way back down

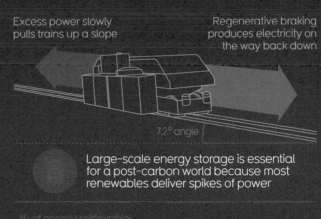

7.2° angle

Large-scale energy storage is essential for a post-carbon world because most renewables deliver spikes of power

% of energy retrievable

TRAINS	80%
FLYWHEELS	80-90%
BATTERIES	75-90%
HYDRO	65-80%
ELECTROTHERMAL	65-75%
COMPRESSED AIR	65-75%

*e.g. water wheels, steam engines, etc

sources: OVO Energy, Energymag

American People Are Very Generous...
Average $ donated per person per year

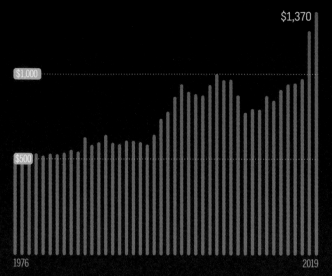

$1,370

$1,000

$500

1976 — 2019

source: Giving USA 2019

...Donating Billions per Year

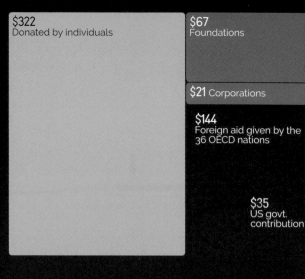

$322
Donated by individuals

$67
Foundations

$21 Corporations

$144
Foreign aid given by the 36 OECD nations

$35
US govt. contribution

sources: Giving USA 2019, OECD

US Prisoner Numbers Are Finally Declining
Yearly increase/decrease

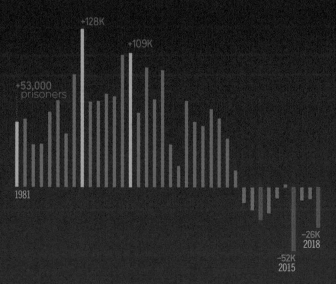

+128K

+109K

+53,000 prisoners

1981

−26K
2018

−52K
2015

source: US Bureau of Justice statistics

Along with Black Incarceration Rates
Variation in % of total prisoners

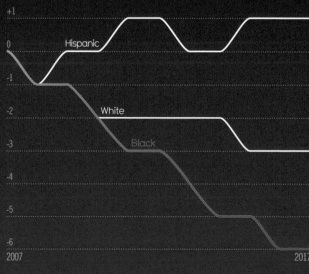

+1

0

Hispanic

-1

-2

White

-3

Black

-4

-5

-6

2007 — 2017

source: US Bureau of Justice statistics

The Average US Citizen Now Lives Much Longer After Retirement

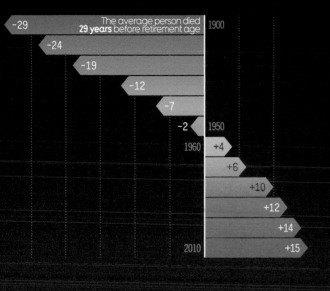

- **-29** 1900 — The average person died **29 years** before retirement age
- **-24**
- **-19**
- **-12**
- **-7**
- **-2** 1950
- 1960 **+4**
- **+6**
- **+10**
- **+12**
- **+14**
- 2010 **+15**

source: Statista

US Recycling is Finally Picking Up

70%

50%

30%

Paper 15% — 67%

34%

26%

Metal 4%
Glass 1%
Plastic 0% — 9%

1970   2018

source: US Environmental Protection Agency

US Teen Pregnancies Have Halved
Births per 1,000 females aged 15-19

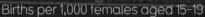

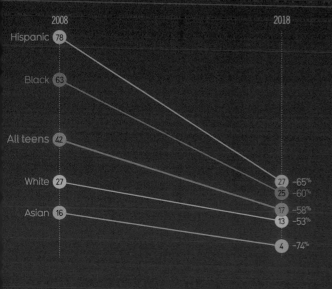

2008	2018
Hispanic 78	27 −65%
Black 63	25 −60%
All teens 42	17 −58%
White 27	13 −53%
Asian 16	4 −74%

sources: Centers for Disease Control, Pew Research Center

US Child Poverty Has Reached an All-Time Low

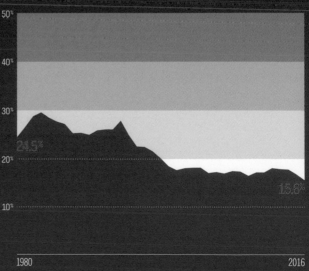

50%

40%

30%

24.5%

20%

15.6%

10%

1980   2016

source: US Department of Agriculture

The US Aims to Halve Food Waste by 2030
A joint effort by institutions, restaurants & grocery stores

America throws out **30–40%** of its food

creating **5–11%** of CO2 emissions

over **$162**bn worth

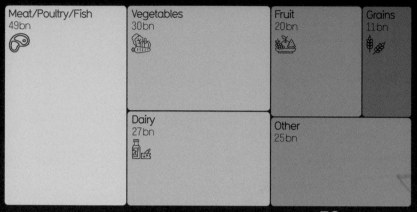

Meat/Poultry/Fish
49bn

Vegetables
30bn

Fruit
20bn

Grains
11bn

Dairy
27bn

Other
25bn

Breakdown by source

Household
61%

Restaurants & food delivery
26%

Retail
12%

that's **58** billion meals

Why is this Happening?

 spoilage insects, rodents, moulds & bacteria

 poor management bad conservation, over-ordering

 customers buy or cook more than needed

 attitude 42% don't have time to consider waste

How will it be fixed?

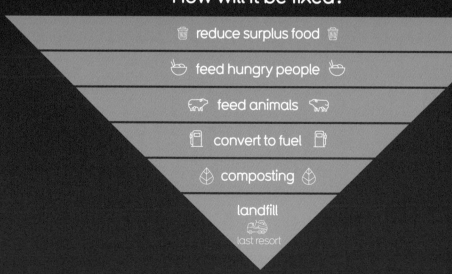

🗑 reduce surplus food 🗑

🍜 feed hungry people 🍜

🐄 feed animals 🐑

⛽ convert to fuel ⛽

🍃 composting 🍃

landfill
last resort

sources: USDA, Rescuing Leftover Cuisine, UNEP, Qi (2016)

HIV / AIDS

The World's No.5 Killer Infection
Infectious disease deaths per day

COVID-19	unknown
Tuberculosis	3,014
Hepatitis B	2,430
Pneumonia	2,216
HIV / AIDS	2,110
Malaria	2,002
Shigellosis	1,644
Rotavirus	1,233
Influenza	1,027
Norovirus	548

source: XXXXX

Claims Nearly 1m Lives Per Year
Million global deaths per year

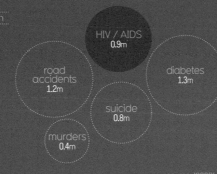

HIV / AIDS
0.9m

road accidents
1.2m

diabetes
1.3m

suicide
0.8m

murders
0.4m

source: XXXXX

Mostly in Southern Africa
Highest deaths

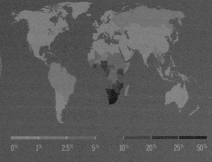

0%   1%   2.5%   5%   10%   20%   25%   50%

source: Our World in Data

But HIV/AIDS Is in Remission Globally
Thanks mainly to widespread anti-viral-drug treatment

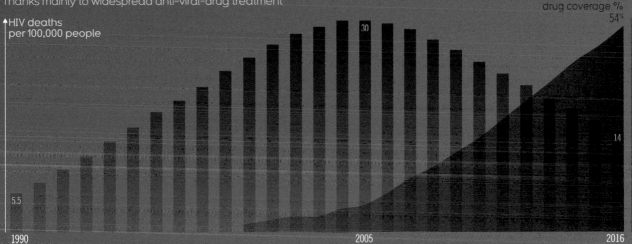

HIV deaths
per 100,000 people

HIV/AIDS
drug coverage %

54%

30

14

5.5

1990   2005   2016

source: Global Health Data Exchange

Prevention of Mother-to-Child HIV Transmission Is Saving Kids

pregnant women with HIV
receiving anti-retroviral meds

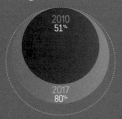

2010
51%

2017
80%

averted child HIV infections
(2010-2018)

1.4 m

• = 1,000 infections

risk of HIV transmission from mother to infant
no treatment   with treatment

15%   45%   <5%

source: Avert.org

Even More Sufferers Are Being Treated
% treated (past & projected)

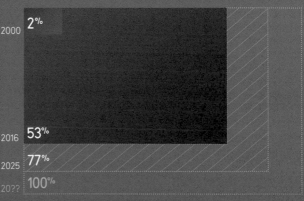

2000	2%
2016	53%
2025	77%
20??	100%

sources: The Lancet, The Guardian

The Potential of Wind Power Is Amazing

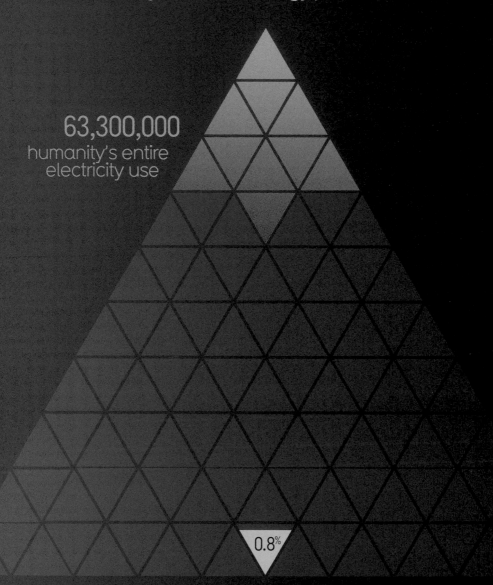

480,000,000
daily megawatt hours
global wind-energy potential

63,300,000
humanity's entire
electricity use

0.8%

amount we're currently using

source: Global Wind Energy Council

It Now Supplies 5% of the World's Energy
and it's growing

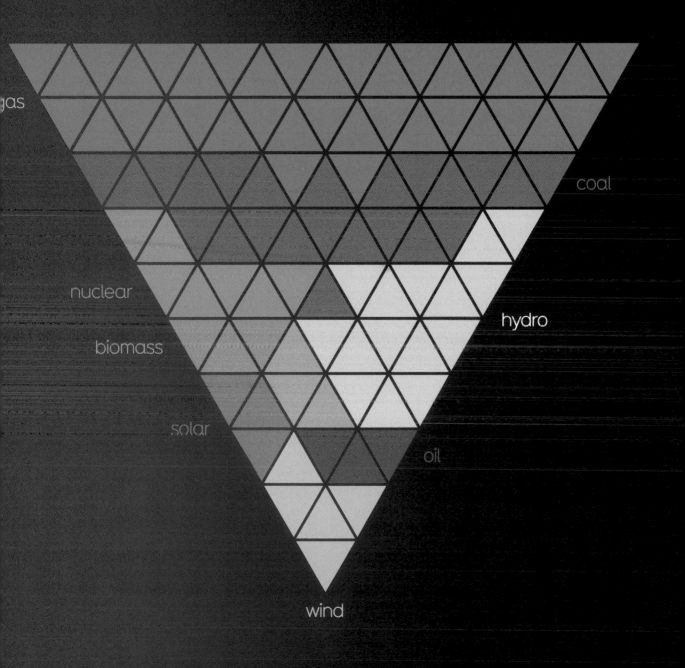

gas

coal

nuclear

hydro

biomass

solar

oil

wind

source: International Energy Agency

Suicide

Global number per 100,000 people

15

-39%

10

5

1994   2019

Declines in some of the worst-suffering countries

Japanese Rate Is the Lowest for 46 Years
Suicides per 100,000 people

Russia Is also At a 50-Year Low

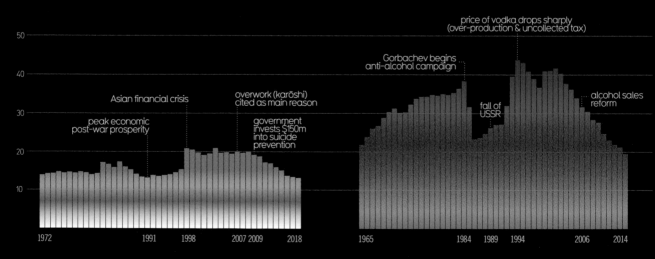

price of vodka drops sharply
(over-production & uncollected tax)

Gorbachev begins
anti-alcohol campaign

50

40

Asian financial crisis

overwork (karōshi)
cited as main reason

alcohol sales
reform

30

peak economic
post-war prosperity

government
invests $150m
into suicide
prevention

fall of
USSR

20

10

1972   1991   1998   2007 2009   2018

1965   1984 1989 1994   2006   2014

sources: Japanese government statistics, New York Times

sources: Human Cause of Death Database, RossSTAT, Moscow

What reduces suicides?

medical   policy   social   cultural

dedicated suicide care on offer

mental health awareness policies & programmes

reducing the stigma of seeking help

strengthening economic security

easier access to mental health support

responsible media reporting

crisis helplines

identification & support of people at risk

community follow-up & group support

restriction in access to means of suicide

reduction in harmful use of alcohol

interventions for vulnerable groups & people

source: Global Health Data Exchange, New York Times

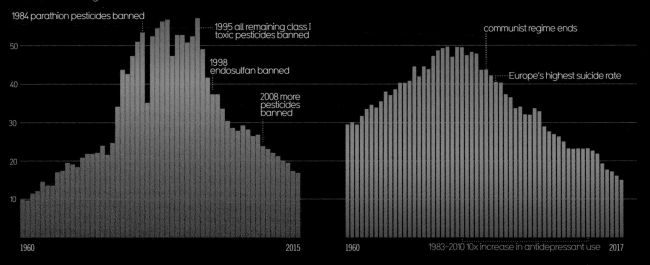

Heartening Declines in Sri Lanka
Had the world's highest suicide rate in 1990

1984 parathion pesticides banned

1995 all remaining class I toxic pesticides banned

1998 endosulfan banned

2008 more pesticides banned

50

40

30

20

10

1960   2015

sources: Worldbank, The Lancet

Hungary Is also Showing a Steady Decline

communist regime ends

Europe's highest suicide rate

1960   1983–2010 10x increase in antidepressant use   2017

source: OECD

Yay Australia!

Australia's Homicide Rate Has Never Been Lower
% variation 1990-2016

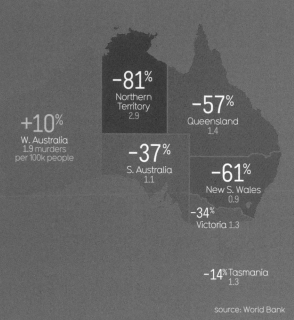

+10%
W. Australia
1.9 murders
per 100k people

−81%
Northern Territory
2.9

−57%
Queensland
1.4

−37%
S. Australia
1.1

−61%
New S. Wales
0.9

−34%
Victoria 1.3

−14% Tasmania
1.3

source: World Bank

On Track to Eradicate Transmission of HIV among Gay Men by End of Decade
Free condoms, clean needles & anti-viral therapy

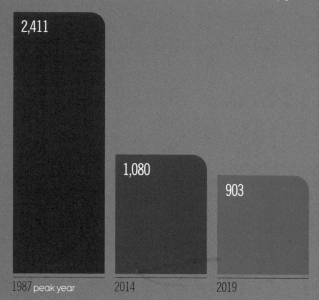

2,411

1,080

903

1987 peak year   2014   2019

sources: Kirby Institute, Guardian

One in Four Australian Homes Now Has Solar Panels

sources: Energy Matters, Australian PV Institute

Government buildings & infrastructure in three major Australian cities are now powered by 100% renewable energy

SYDNEY   MELBOURNE   ADELAIDE

street lights, government buildings, swimming pools, sports fields

75% wind, 25% solar

source: PV Magazine

Aboriginal Australians Are Now Empowered to Reduce Wildfires
using ancient indigenous techniques

Defensive burning is a fire-prevention strategy

Strategic small fires reduce undergrowth that can fuel bigger blazes

$80 million

Given to organisations that practise defensive burning

−40% greenhouse gases

Fewer fires, fewer emissionsthanks to these techniques

source: New York Times

Australia Has a Mobile Shower and Laundry Service for the Homeless
It focuses on empathetic, positive connections

116,000
homeless in Australia (1 in 200 adults)

134,000
loads of washing

13,000
âtaken

212,000
hours of conversation

1,700
registered volunteers

23
cities around Australia

source: OrangeSky.org.au. per year

Building the most ambitious renewable energy project ever
The Australian-Singapore power link

WORLD'S LARGEST SOLAR FARM	WORLD'S LARGEST BATTERY	transporting energy to Singapore via..	...WORLD'S LONGEST UNDERSEA CABLE	TOTAL INVESTMENT

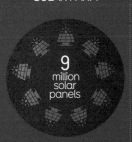

9 million solar panels

30GWh

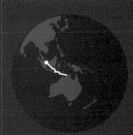

Australia to Singapore
3,700km

730km
Norway to UK cable

$16 billion

10GW

Buzen Substation Battery (Japan) 300MWh

2.2GW

1.4GW

1,500jobs

enough for a small country or 10 mid-sized cities

Hornsdale (Australia) 193MWh

20% of Singapore's electricity use per year

$750 million export revenue per year

sources: SunCable.sg, US Dollars

Magic Materials

PLANT   ANIMAL   MINERAL

Gulam

Short for 'glued laminated timber'.
One of the highest available
strength-to-weight ratios.

CONSTRUCTION   BUILDINGS

Totally renewable & recyclable
Strength can vary, also expensive

Shrilk

Leftover shrimp shells & silk proteins.
As strong as aluminium, but
half the weight.

MEDICAL   PACKAGING

Totally biodegradable
Limited supply of raw materials

Hemp

Ancient, very fast-growing woven-
fibre material derived from cannabis.
Huge variety of uses.

TEXTILES   PAPER   CLOTHING

Lightweight & breathable
Illegal in some nations due to cannabis laws

Nanocellulose

Tiny non-toxic fibres from
ground-up wood pulp are 10 times
stronger than steel.

PACKAGING   FURNITURE   CLOTHING

extremely versatile, totally biodegrable
requires a lot of energy to produce

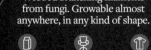

Mycelium

Webbed branching filaments
from fungi. Growable almost
anywhere, in any kind of shape.

PACKAGING   FURNITURE   CLOTHING

Extremely versatile, already in production
None!

Aerogels

Lightest known material. A rigid, ultralight foam with excellent heat and sound insulation.

INSULATION   BUILDING

Extremely versatile
Very brittle – shatters under high pressure

Carbon Nanotubes

Layers of carbon atoms rolled into cylinders with extraordinary thermal & electrical properties.

SENSORS   TRANSISTORS   BATTERIES

100x stronger than steel, 6x lighter
Tricky to create large amounts

Bioconcrete

Mixing sand, water, microbes and calcium creates a stone-like substance with low eco-impact.

CONSTRUCTION

Concrete is a major source of emissions
Process needs scaling up

Hyaline

AI-developed flexible, transparent, cellophane-like bio-electronic film, made via bacterial fermentation.

FOLDABLE PHONES   WEARABLES

Amazingly flexible & recyclable
Already patented & commercialised

Graphene

A single-atom-thick sheet of carbon with incredible flexibility & strength.

ELECTRONICS

Transparent & electrically conductive
Proving difficult to scale up

Stone Wool

Igneous rock and slag from steelmaking, when melted together, can be spun into versatile fibres.

INSULATION

Great for eco-conscious building
Protective gear required

sources: BBC, HuffPost, Nature (journal), NASA Jet Propulsion Lab, ACS, Forbes

The world ha
fourth type c

beyond

DARK
WHITE
MILK

there's now RUBY

gained a
chocolate...

Ruby chocolate, invented in 2017 by
Belgian-Swiss confectioner Barry Callebaut,
is made from unfermented cocoa beans.
The exact process is a trade secret, but the
result is a "sweet yet sour" taste: milkier than
dark, fruitier than milk, and even sweeter
than white chocolate.

Renewable Energy

Costs Are Falling Fast
Decrease in price 2017 to 2018

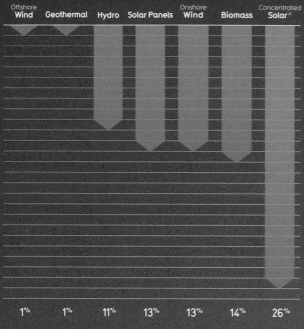

Offshore Wind	Geothermal	Hydro	Solar Panels	Onshore Wind	Biomass	Concentrated Solar*
1%	1%	11%	13%	13%	14%	26%

* uses mirrors to focus sunlight to power a generator

source: IRENA.org

Renewables Are Rapidly Outpacing Coal

Global energy production
(gigawatts)

2,200

2008 — 2017

sources: International Renewable Energy Agency, Carbon Brief

Global Investment Is Rising...

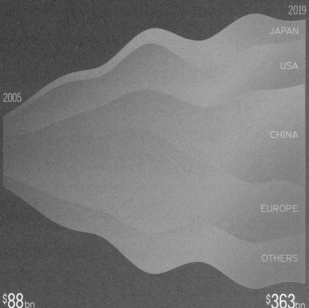

2019
JAPAN
USA
CHINA
EUROPE
OTHERS

2005

$88bn

$363bn

source: World Bank

...To Twice as Much as Fossil Fuels
$billion power sector investment

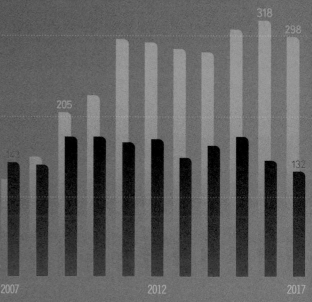

318
298
205
143
132

2007 — 2012 — 2017

source: International Energy Agency

Renewable Energy Superstars

% of electricity from renewables

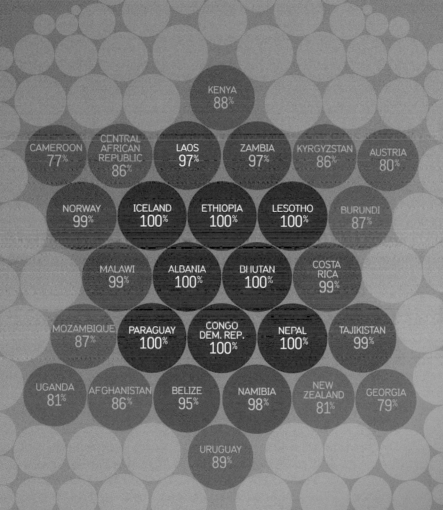

KENYA 88%

CAMEROON 77%
CENTRAL AFRICAN REPUBLIC 86%
LAOS 97%
ZAMBIA 97%
KYRGYZSTAN 86%
AUSTRIA 80%

NORWAY 99%
ICELAND 100%
ETHIOPIA 100%
LESOTHO 100%
BURUNDI 87%

MALAWI 99%
ALBANIA 100%
BHUTAN 100%
COSTA RICA 99%

MOZAMBIQUE 87%
PARAGUAY 100%
CONGO DEM. REP. 100%
NEPAL 100%
TAJIKISTAN 99%

UGANDA 81%
AFGHANISTAN 86%
BELIZE 95%
NAMIBIA 98%
NEW ZEALAND 81%
GEORGIA 79%

URUGUAY 89%

source: International Energy Agency

Fairphone 3 Is a Sustainable Alternative to Polluting Smartphones

Reducing electronic waste & improving workers' conditions

Smartphones Are a Major Contributor to Electronic Waste

rare materials
extraction process is
energy-intensive;
recycling is hard

obsolescence
impossible to
replace components,
only entire phone

strong glue
makes it difficult
to disassemble,
fix or recycle

E-Waste Produced per Person per year

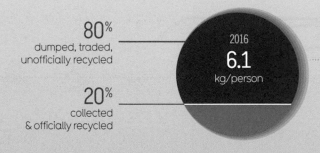

80%
dumped, traded,
unofficially recycled

20%
collected
& officially recycled

2016
6.1
kg/person

2021
6.8kg
11% increase

the fate of most
e-waste is unknown

Fairphone 3

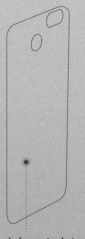

replaceable battery
no need for assistance

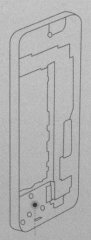

modular design
fixing & upgrading
is simpler & cheaper

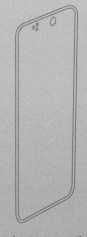

fair materials
recycled plastics
& copper; Fairtrade gold

screws, not glue
for quick replacement
of components

ethical production
manufacturer guarantees
workers' rights

sources: Dezeen.com, United Nations University

We Are Winning the Fight Against Tuberculosis (TB)

TB Deaths Are Falling Worldwide

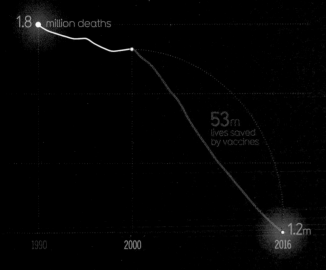

1.8 million deaths

53m lives saved by vaccines

1.2m

1990   2000   2016

It's One of the World's Biggest Killer Diseases
Average global disease deaths per day

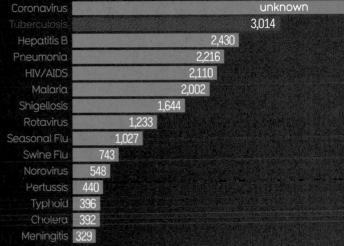

Disease	Deaths per day
Coronavirus	unknown
Tuberculosis	3,014
Hepatitis B	2,430
Pneumonia	2,216
HIV/AIDS	2,110
Malaria	2,002
Shigellosis	1,644
Rotavirus	1,233
Seasonal Flu	1,027
Swine Flu	743
Norovirus	548
Pertussis	440
Typhoid	396
Cholera	392
Meningitis	329

90%+ of Children Are Now Vaccinated
In over 100 vulnerable countries

The Deadliest Form of TB Is Now Curable
Cure rate of extensively drug-resistant strain (XDR)

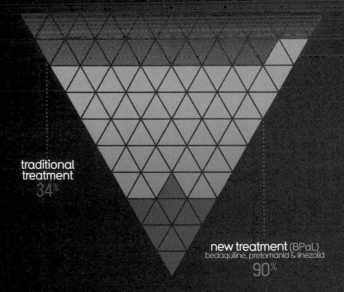

traditional treatment
34%

new treatment (BPaL)
bedaquiline, pretomanid & linezolid
90%

sources: New York Times, Centers for Disease Control, Global Burden of Disease Collaborative Network, World Health Organisation

South Korea is Solving Its Massive Food Waste Problem

S. Koreans generate
a huge volume
of food waste

It's even bigger
than **Europe** and
North America

130
kg/year
per person

average
105
kg/year

the solution

**ban on dumping
food in landfill**

**compulsory
food recycling**

using special
biodegradable bags

average monthly
bag cost per family

bags fund most
of the scheme

$6

60%

the results

Food Waste Recycled

1995

2019

2%

95%

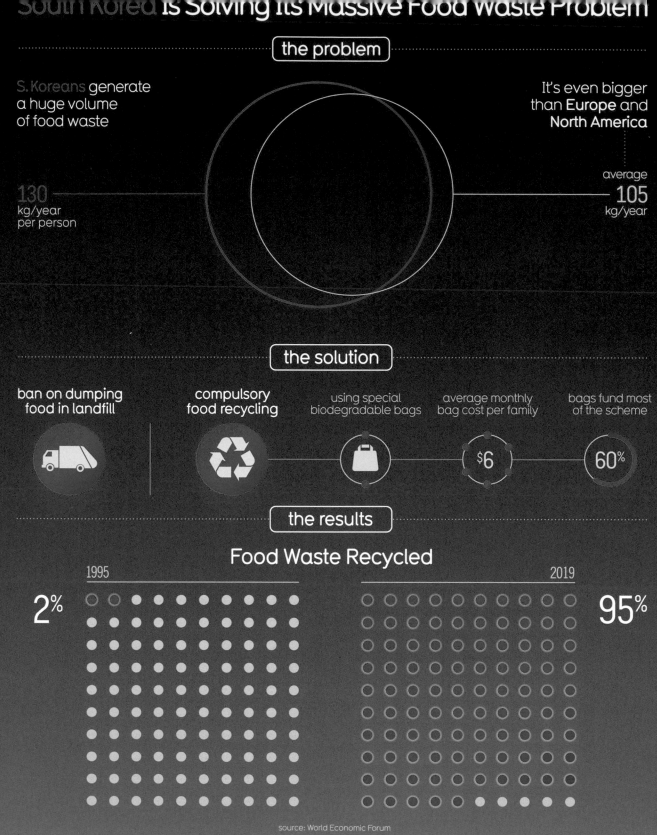

source: World Economic Forum

Numbers of Infections

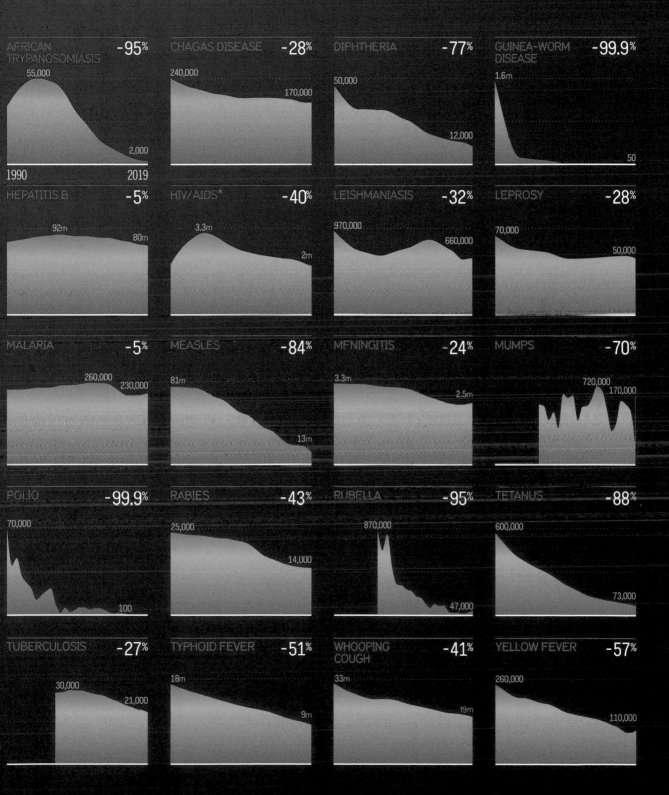

AFRICAN TRYPANOSOMIASIS	-95%

55,000

2,000

1990 — 2019

CHAGAS DISEASE	-28%

240,000

170,000

DIPHTHERIA	-77%

50,000

12,000

GUINEA-WORM DISEASE	-99.9%

1.6m

50

HEPATITIS B	-5%

92m

80m

HIV/AIDS*	-40%

3.3m

2m

LEISHMANIASIS	-32%

970,000

660,000

LEPROSY	-28%

70,000

50,000

MALARIA	-5%

260,000

230,000

MEASLES	-84%

81m

13m

MENINGITIS	-24%

3.3m

2.5m

MUMPS	-70%

720,000

170,000

POLIO	-99.9%

70,000

100

RABIES	-43%

25,000

14,000

RUBELLA	-95%

870,000

47,000

TETANUS	-88%

600,000

73,000

TUBERCULOSIS	-27%

30,000

21,000

TYPHOID FEVER	-51%

18m

9m

WHOOPING COUGH	-41%

33m

19m

YELLOW FEVER	-57%

260,000

110,000

source: World Health Organisation, IHME, World Bank * = decline from peak

Global Tree Cover Is Expanding

Gain and loss of tree canopy cover 1982–2016

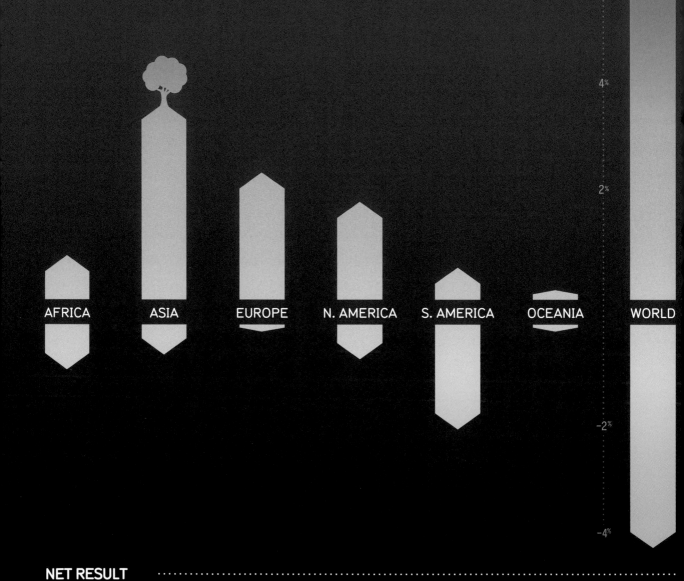

8%

6%

4%

2%

AFRICA ASIA EUROPE N. AMERICA S. AMERICA OCEANIA WORLD

-2%

-4%

NET RESULT

-0.1%   +11.7%   +27.3%   +6.5%   -4.9%   +2.4%   +5.4%

source: Global Land Change from 1962–2016, Song et al (2018)

Life Expectancy in Africa Is Soaring

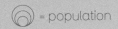 = population

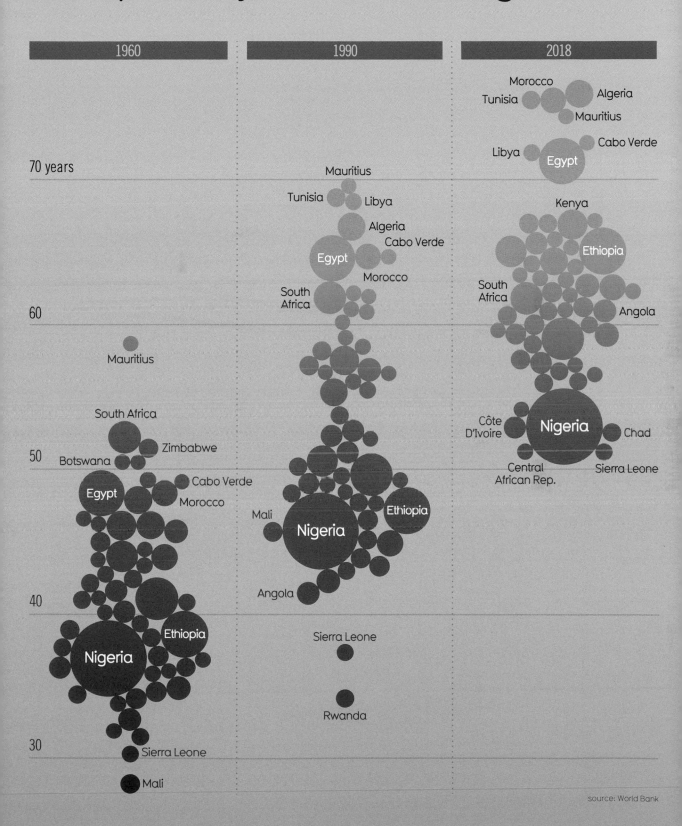

| 1960 | 1990 | 2018 |

70 years

60

50

40

30

1960
Mauritius
South Africa
Zimbabwe
Botswana
Cabo Verde
Egypt
Morocco
Nigeria
Ethiopia
Sierra Leone
Mali

1990
Mauritius
Tunisia
Libya
Algeria
Cabo Verde
Egypt
Morocco
South Africa
Mali
Nigeria
Ethiopia
Angola
Sierra Leone
Rwanda

2018
Morocco
Tunisia
Algeria
Mauritius
Libya
Egypt
Cabo Verde
Kenya
Ethiopia
South Africa
Angola
Côte D'Ivoire
Nigeria
Chad
Central African Rep.
Sierra Leone

source: World Bank

China is...

Eradicating Extreme Poverty
People living on less than $1.90 per day

7m
2016

1990
756m

source: World Bank

Pioneering the Electric Bus

98% of the world's electric buses

0.5 million in operation

source: V

Crushing Demand for Ivory

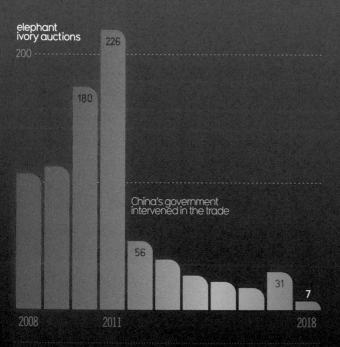

elephant
ivory auctions

200

226

180

China's government
intervened in the trade

56

31

7

2008   2011   2018

source: Traffic

A World Leader in Electric Cars

	China	USA
electric cars produced	1.2m	325,000
fast electric car chargers	310,000	17,000
that's one charger for every...	**12** cars	**94**

source: Bloomberg

Especially in places like Shenzhen
China's 6th biggest city (population 12 million)

100% first all-electric bus fleet

16,000 e-buses

1,700 chargers

across **104** locations

48% less CO2 emissions

26 million tonnes of CO2 saved

sources: Bloomberg NEF, International Energy Agency

Aiming to Generate Half Its Energy from Renewables by 2040

3,188 GW

1,625 gigawatts

	2016	2040
renewables	35%	57%
fossil fuel & nuclear	65%	43%

source: International Energy Agency

Winning Its War on Air Pollution
Fine particulate matter (PM 2.5) reduction (selected regions)

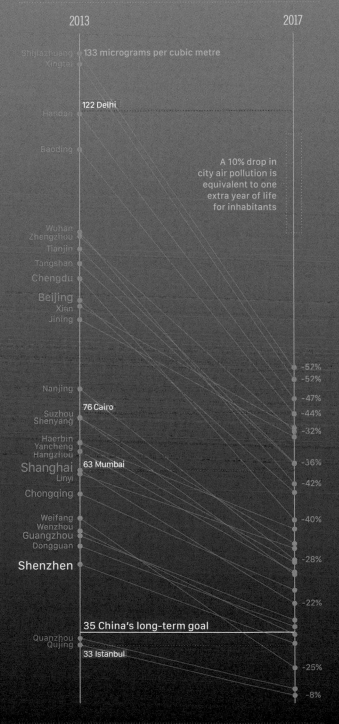

2013 — 2017

Shijiazhuang
Xingtai
133 micrograms per cubic metre

122 Delhi

Handan

Baoding

A 10% drop in city air pollution is equivalent to one extra year of life for inhabitants

Wuhan
Zhengzhou
Tianjin
Tangshan
Chengdu
Beijing
Xian
Jining

Nanjing
76 Cairo

Suzhou
Shenyang

Haerbin
Yancheng
Hangzhou
Shanghai
63 Mumbai
Linyi

Chongqing

Weifang
Wenzhou
Guangzhou
Dongguan

Shenzhen

35 China's long-term goal
Quanzhou
Qujing
33 Istanbul

-52%
-52%
-47%
-44%
-32%
-36%
-42%
-40%
-28%
-22%
-25%
-8%

sources: Energy Policy Institute at the University of Chicago, Guardian

We're Eliminating Malaria Worldwide
Countries certified malaria-free

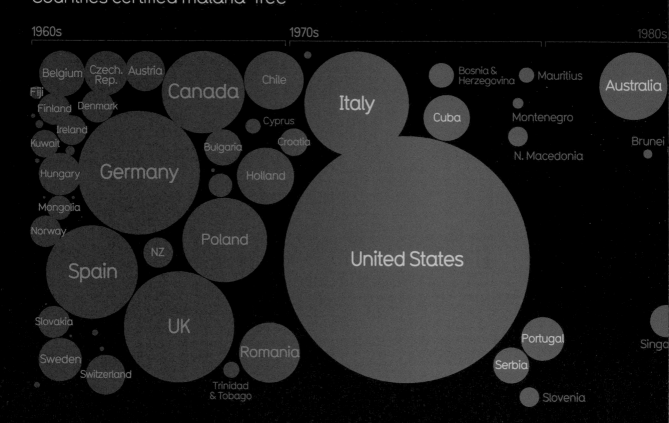

◎ = population

1960s   1970s   1980s

Belgium, Czech. Rep., Austria, Fiji, Finland, Denmark, Ireland, Kuwait, Hungary, Mongolia, Norway, Germany, Canada, Chile, Cyprus, Bulgaria, Croatia, Holland, NZ, Poland, Spain, Italy, United States, Slovakia, UK, Sweden, Switzerland, Trinidad & Tobago, Romania, Bosnia & Herzegovina, Cuba, Mauritius, Montenegro, N. Macedonia, Australia, Brunei, Portugal, Serbia, Slovenia, Singa[pore]

Fewer Children Are Dying
Thousands of deaths per year

627 — 2004
545 — 2007
431 — 2010
323 — 2013
288 — 2016

Simple bed nets have prevented **half a billion** malaria infections

source: United Nations Children's Fund (UNICEF)

source: Our World in Data

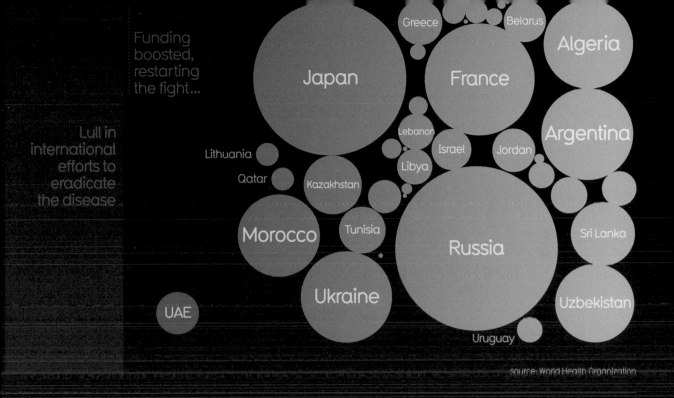

Funding
boosted,
restarting
the fight...

Lull in
international
efforts to
eradicate
the disease

Greece   Belarus

Japan

France

Algeria

Lithuania

Qatar

Kazakhstan

Lebanon

Israel

Libya

Jordan

Argentina

Morocco

Tunisia

Russia

Sri Lanka

Ukraine

Uzbekistan

UAE

Uruguay

source: World Health Organization

Global Deaths Are Falling

930,000 ●   70+ years old

50–69

● 670,000

15–49

5–14

620,000 ●

under 5s

1990   2003   2016

source: Our World in Data

How do we solve our PLASTICS problem?

- pollution
- microplastics
- carbon emissions
- poor biodegradability

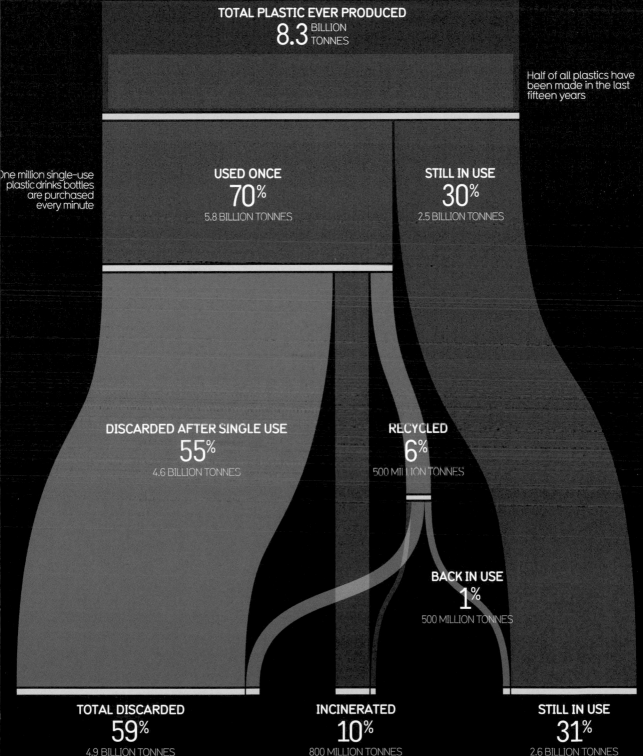

TOTAL PLASTIC EVER PRODUCED
8.3 BILLION TONNES

Half of all plastics have been made in the last fifteen years

One million single-use plastic drinks bottles are purchased every minute

USED ONCE
70%
5.8 BILLION TONNES

STILL IN USE
30%
2.5 BILLION TONNES

DISCARDED AFTER SINGLE USE
55%
4.6 BILLION TONNES

RECYCLED
6%
500 MILLION TONNES

BACK IN USE
1%
500 MILLION TONNES

TOTAL DISCARDED
59%
4.9 BILLION TONNES

INCINERATED
10%
800 MILLION TONNES

STILL IN USE
31%
2.6 BILLION TONNES

Main Types of Plastic

PLASTIC	PET	HDPE	PVC	LDPE	PP	PS	other
	1	2	3	4	5	6	7
NAME	Polyethylene Terephthalate	High-Density Polyethylene	Polyvinyl Chloride	Low-Density Polyethylene	Polypropylene	Polystyrene	many different plastics
AKA	polyester, PETE	polythene	vinyl			Styrofoam	
USES	water & fizzy drink bottles, combs, shampoo, food and medicine containers	milk & juice bottles, some shopping bags, shampoo & detergent & bleach bottles, some toys	plumbing pipes, some grocery bags, clingfilm, shoes	plastic bags, disposable gloves, clingfilm, squeezable bottles (like mustard)	nappies/diapers, straws, yoghurt pots, prescription bottles, pegs, ice cream tubs, plant pots	disposable coffee cups, plastic cutlery, some toys, coat hangers	baby bottles, eye glasses, plastic furniture
PROPERTIES	clear, very tough	crinkles to touch, floats	transparent, strong	soft, flexible but tough	heat-resistant	brittle, glassy, insulating	multiple
% OF PRODUCTION	9%	14%	10%	17%	18%	6%	26%
AMOUNT IN ENVIRONMENT	11.2%	14%	5.3%	20%	19.3%	6%	24.2%
RECYCLABILITY	HIGH	HIGH	NO	HIGH	MEDIUM	LOW	MIXED

BIODEGRADABLE?	NO	NO	NO	NO	NO	some
HEALTH & SAFETY	mixed odours & flavours leak in, do not reuse	no no contact with food or drink, leaks chemicals	safe	safe	no affected by fats, never use as food storage, extremely toxic	usually not healthy, do not use store food
COMMON WASTE	most single-use plastic waste		food wrappers, grocery bags	bottle tops, straws	majority of ocean waste	
PYROLYSIS see page ▶ 000	NO	NO	YES	YES	MAYBE	MAYBE

POPULARITY ◀ ·········

	NAME	AKA	USES
PUR	Polyurethane	spandex, lycra	clothing
PC	Polycarbonate		compact discs, eye-glass lenses, riot shields
PMMA	Polymethylmethacrylate	perspex, acrylic	contact lenses, glazing, paints
PA	Polyamides	nylon	clothing, tyres, ropes, toothbrush bristles
PTFE	Polytetrafluoroethylene	teflon	non-stick frying pans, plumber's tape
PCL	Polycaprolactone 🌎 = biodegradable	bio-polyester	clothing, glues
ABS	Acrylonitrile butadiene styrene		lego, computer keyboards, printers
PVDC	Polyvinylidene chloride	saran, clingfilm	packaging
XPS	Extruded polystyrene		insulation
PF	Phenol formaldehyde	bakelite	foam, mouldings, billiard balls
POM	Polyoxymethylene	acetal	gears, industrial uses
MF	Melamine formaldehyde		children's cups & plates
SAN	Styrene acrylonitrile		food containers, kitchenware, packaging
APET	Amorphous PET		water bottles
PBA	Polybutyrate		paper cups
PBS	Polybutylene succinate 🌎		agriculture
CPET	Crystaline PET		microwave containers

sources: Guardian, Our World in Data

The properties
that make plastics
so versatile & useful
also make them
difficult or impossible
for nature to fully
assimilate

'Biodegradable' **Plastics**

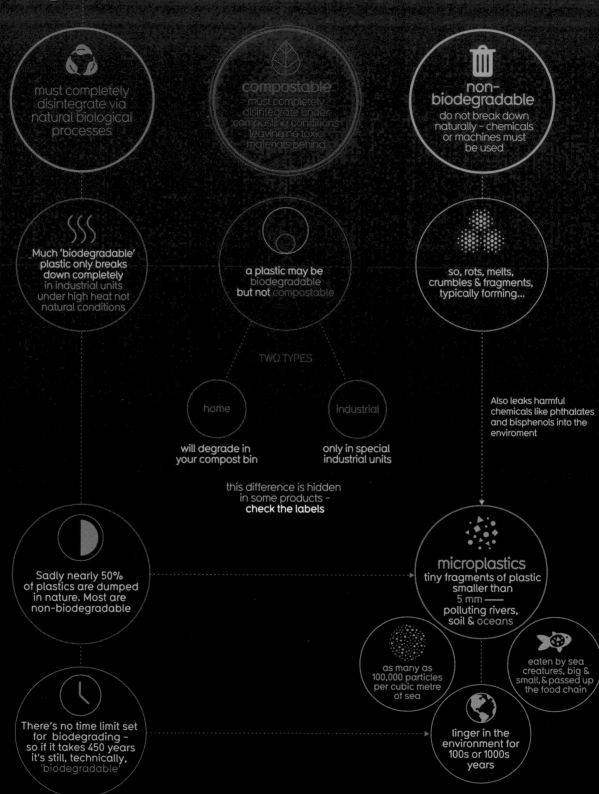

must completely disintegrate via natural biological processes

compostable
must completely disintegrate under composting conditions leaving no toxic materials behind

non-biodegradable
do not break down naturally – chemicals or machines must be used

Much 'biodegradable' plastic only breaks down completely in industrial units under high heat not natural conditions

a plastic may be biodegradable but not compostable

so, rots, melts, crumbles & fragments, typically forming...

TWO TYPES

home
will degrade in your compost bin

industrial
only in special industrial units

Also leaks harmful chemicals like phthalates and bisphenols into the enviroment

this difference is hidden in some products – **check the labels**

Sadly nearly 50% of plastics are dumped in nature. Most are non-biodegradable

microplastics
tiny fragments of plastic smaller than 5 mm ——— polluting rivers, soil & oceans

as many as 100,000 particles per cubic metre of sea

eaten by sea creatures, big & small, & passed up the food chain

There's no time limit set for biodegrading – so if it takes 450 years it's still, technically, 'biodegradable'

linger in the environment for 100s or 1000s years

sources: NPR, National Geographic, Wiethmann et al (2018), New York Times

Can't we just use bioplastics instead?

plastics not made from fossil fuels like oil
instead come from 'bio', potentially renewable sources like:

 starch

 wood pulp

 proteins

 sugars

 crop residues

Watch out for marketing terms like 'plant-based', 'bio-based' or 'compostable'

Any plastic derived from these sources can be called a 'bioplastic'

But those sources aren't necessarily biodegradable, compostable or even ecofriendly

⊕ PROS

usually more sustainable

80% less energy usage

80% less emissions

fewer toxins released in production

several are biodegradable

a few are compostable

⊖ CONS

extra land, water to grow materials

more fertiliser used

not as strong or versatile as normal plastics

chemical additives still used (dyes, fillers, coatings)

broadly no more biodegradable than normal plastics

not always recyclable in usual recycling streams

What *are* they good for?

food service	foil packaging	diapers/ nappies	fruit & veg packaging	tyres	mulch foils	bags
25%	22%	17%	11%	11%	7%	6%

Current usage

1% of all plastics

Popular & emerging bio-plastics

	PRIMARY SOURCE	USES	♻ 🌐 🏭 🏠 🔥	NOTE
TPS	maize starch	films, bags, cutlery, packaging	* ● ● ● ●	starch is abundant & renewable
PLA	corn starch	3D printing, cups, nappies, teabags	● ● ● ● ●	can replace PS(6), PP(5), ABS
PHB	glucose	transparent films	● ● ● ● ?	may replace PVC(3) & LDPE (4)
PHA	sugars	packaging, films, straws, bottles	? ● ● ● ●	very promising, replaces PP, tricky to scale
bioPE	ethanol	water bottles	* ○ ○ ● ●	identical to PE just not fossil-fuel
PEF	sugars	bottles, films, food trays	* ● ● ● ?	shows promise
plantic	corn starch	food packaging	* ● ● ● ?	great food packaging, home compostable

(good) ♻ recyclable ● separate stream req. 🌐 biodegradable 🏭 industrially compost 🏠 home compost 🔥 heat resistant (good for packaging)

sources: Wikipedia, Forbes, US Environmental Protection Agency, Broeren (2017), Yale School of the Environment

Most Plastic Waste

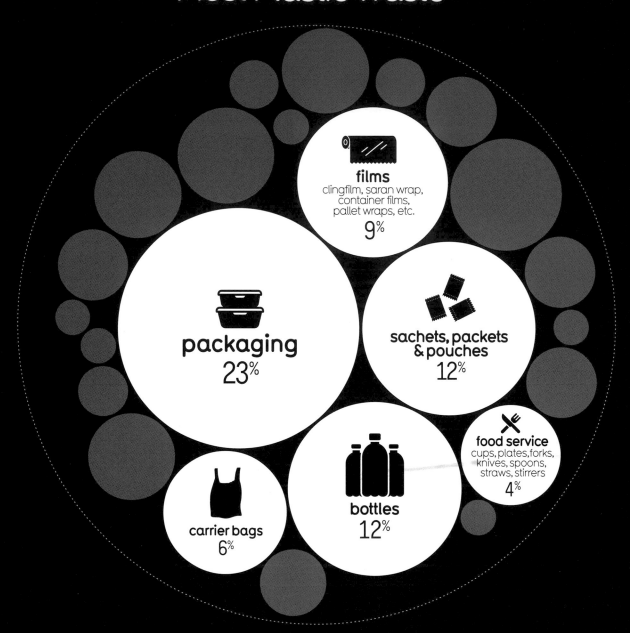

films
clingfilm, saran wrap, container films, pallet wraps, etc.
9%

packaging
23%

sachets, packets & pouches
12%

food service
cups, plates, forks, knives, spoons, straws, stirrers
4%

carrier bags
6%

bottles
12%

Most Dumped on Beaches

8%
cutlery

9%
food containers

13%
bags

22%
cigarette butts

10%
caps, lids

4%
bottles

4%
ropes, string

Marine Debris Decomposition Time

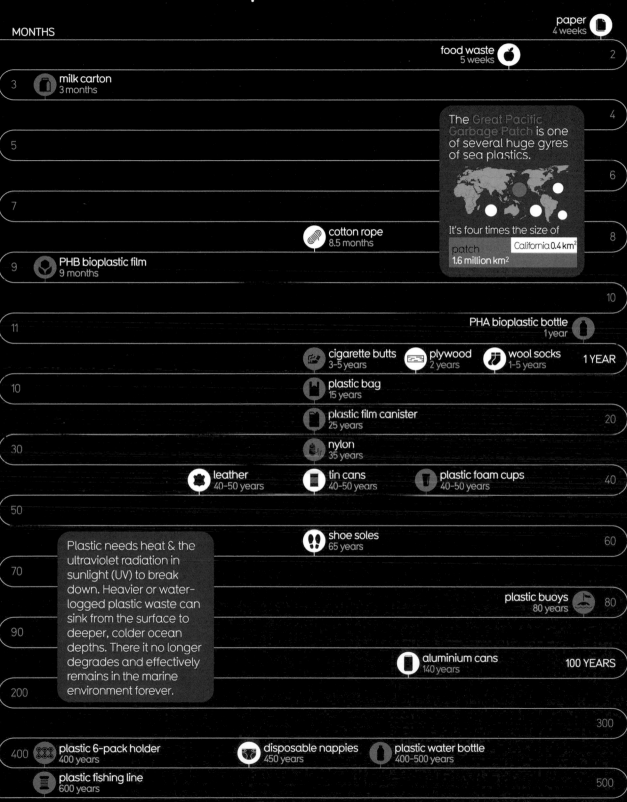

plastic   other material

MONTHS

paper 4 weeks

food waste 5 weeks — 2

3 **milk carton** 3 months

4

5

6

7

The Great Pacific Garbage Patch is one of several huge gyres of sea plastics.

It's four times the size of

patch **1.6 million km²** California 0.4 km²

cotton rope 8.5 months — 8

9 **PHB bioplastic film** 9 months

10

11 **PHA bioplastic bottle** 1 year

cigarette butts 3–5 years   **plywood** 2 years   **wool socks** 1–5 years   **1 YEAR**

10 **plastic bag** 15 years

plastic film canister 25 years — 20

30 **nylon** 35 years

leather 40–50 years   **tin cans** 40–50 years   **plastic foam cups** 40–50 years — 40

50

shoe soles 65 years — 60

70

Plastic needs heat & the ultraviolet radiation in sunlight (UV) to break down. Heavier or water-logged plastic waste can sink from the surface to deeper, colder ocean depths. There it no longer degrades and effectively remains in the marine environment forever.

plastic buoys 80 years — 80

90

aluminium cans 140 years   **100 YEARS**

200

300

400 **plastic 6-pack holder** 400 years   **disposable nappies** 450 years   **plastic water bottle** 400–500 years

plastic fishing line 600 years — 500

sources: Our World in Data, Ocean Conservancy.org

Our Routes for Solving Plastics

THICKNESS = IMPACT

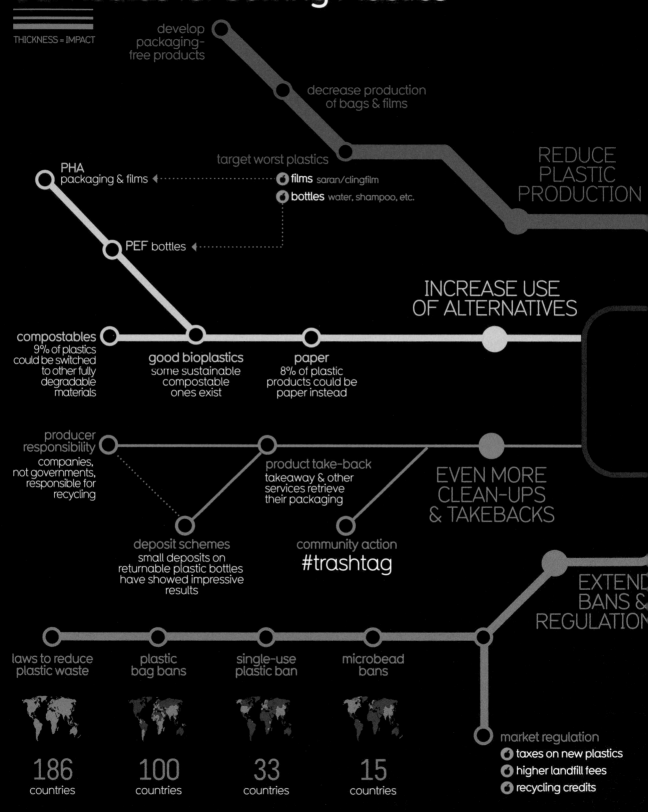

develop packaging-free products

decrease production of bags & films

REDUCE PLASTIC PRODUCTION

target worst plastics

PHA packaging & films ◄

◉ **films** saran/clingfilm
◉ **bottles** water, shampoo, etc.

PEF bottles ◄

INCREASE USE OF ALTERNATIVES

compostables
9% of plastics could be switched to other fully degradable materials

good bioplastics
some sustainable compostable ones exist

paper
8% of plastic products could be paper instead

producer responsibility
companies, not governments, responsible for recycling

product take-back
takeaway & other services retrieve their packaging

EVEN MORE CLEAN-UPS & TAKEBACKS

deposit schemes
small deposits on returnable plastic bottles have showed impressive results

community action
#trashtag

EXTEND BANS & REGULATION

laws to reduce plastic waste

plastic bag bans

single-use plastic ban

microbead bans

186 countries

100 countries

33 countries

15 countries

market regulation
◉ taxes on new plastics
◉ higher landfill fees
◉ recycling credits

double mechanical recycling to

42 ↑ 85
MILLION TONNES

increase collection & recycling infrastructure

% plastic packaging recycled

EU ▬▬▬▬▬ 42%
USA ▬▬ 8%

BETTER & INCREASED RECYCLING

support global recycling

50%+
ocean plastic comes from global south

scale up in recycling in those nations

especially of commonly dumped plastic bottles

make recycling profitable
currently landfill is more economical

remove pigments
zero dyes can increase recycling value by
25%

design for recycling
many items are still difficult, uneconomical or impossible to recycle

MORE REUSE & REPURPOSING

multi-use items
replace single-use products with reusable items owned by the user

- ● water bottles
- ● coffee cups
- ● cutlery
- ● plastic bags

refill shops & systems
water, shampoo oils, sauces from dispensers by default

CURVEBALLS & NEW TECH

PTO

THINKING CIRCULAR

plastic pollution is a by-product
of the unsustainable linear economy of high-income nations

forge a circular plastics system
deriving revenue from circulation of materials rather than wasting & dumping

REDUCE PLASTIC WASTE

expand waste collection rates
+90% urban areas
+50% rural

support plastic pickers
improve conditions for the
11 MILLION PLASTIC PICKERS
responsible for
60% OF GLOBAL RECYCLING

reduce open burning
65 MILLION TONNES
of plastic waste just burnt (20%)

3.5 MILLION TONNES
10-20% lost or leaked

reduce maritime sources
fishing lines & nets are 10-30% of ocean pollution

controlled disposal
23% CANNOT BE RECYCLED

reduce/end waste exports
to middle- or low-income countries

sources: New York Times, Yale School of the Environment

Creative Solutions

Pyrolysis converts used, unrecyclable waste back into plastic & energy

what is it?
a chemical process that breaks plastic back down into its molecular building blocks

major impact
chemical conversion could recycle 26 million tonnes per year (up from 1.4m today)

double recycling
plastics that are too contaminated or can't be mechanically recycled can undergo pyrolysis

infinite recycling
potentially a plastic can go through pyrolysis over and over again, ad infinitum

Pyrolysis is an early-stage technology, so accurate data on its impact & contributions is still emerging

source: PEW

Bespoke Enzymes Can Turn Major Plastics into Biodegradables

catalytic enzyme added as pellets to plastic resin at point of manufacture

after a dormancy period, enzymes kick in and digest the plastic into wax

the wax attracts and is edible by microbes, fungi & bacteria which consume it

dissolves both to water, CO2 and organic material in less than a year

works on world's leading non-biodegradable plastics **polyethylene (PET)** and **polypropylene (PP)**

PET

PP

Doesn't work on landfill. Only works on dumped plastic. On land & not in the ocean.

source: Polymateria.com

Six Organic, Biodegradable Alternatives to Single-Use Plastics

seaweed extract
a jelly (agar) made from the
fast-growing sea plant
(replaces **bags**)

fish scales
waste from food factories
bound with algae
(packaging)

cellulose nanofibres
tiny, crystalline molecules
extracted from wood pulp
(styrofoam)

hemp
tough, super-versatile
material from cannabis plants
(bottles)

elephant grass
a low-cost, hardy, fibrous
African plant
(packaging)

mycelium
thread-like roots of mushrooms
bound into plant material
(styrofoam)

sources: Wired, CNN, Washington State University

We're Developing & Harnessing Natural Organisms & Substances That Can Eat & Digest Plastic Waste

bacteria
breaks the plastic down & uses it
as energy as fuel for further digestion

fungi
promising & already in use but much
harder to harness on an industrial scale

enzymes
mutant bacterial enzyme (PET hydrolase)
can easily metabolise plastic in hours

mealworms
microorganisms in the guts of the darkling
beetle larvae break down plastic

PUR
Polyurethane
e.g. sneakers,
nappies, sponges

PET
Polyethylene
bottles, food
containers

PS
Polystyrene
disposable cups &
glasses, packaging

sources: European Commission, Nature (journal), Stanford University

What can you do?
Simple actions to take in your everyday life

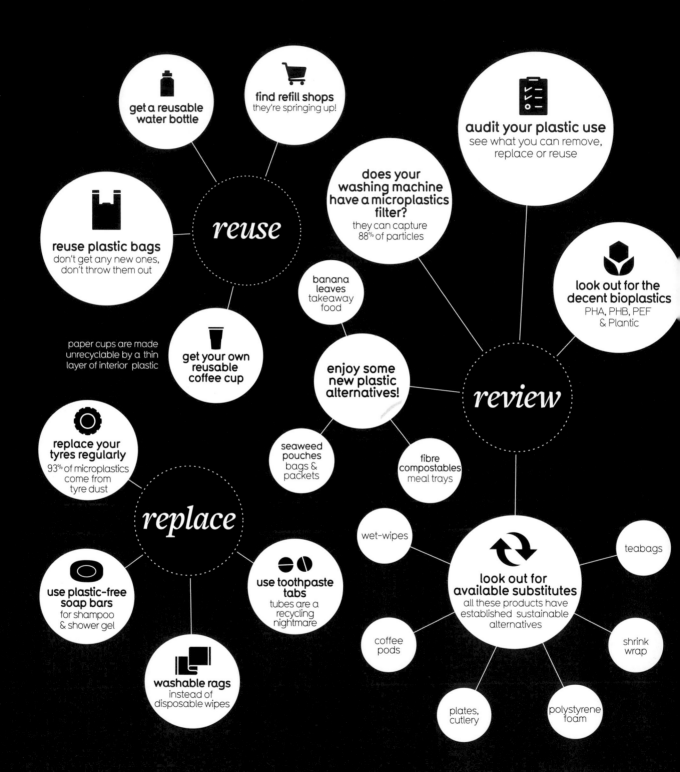

get a reusable water bottle

find refill shops
they're springing up!

audit your plastic use
see what you can remove, replace or reuse

reuse

does your washing machine have a microplastics filter?
they can capture 88% of particles

look out for the decent bioplastics
PHA, PHB, PEF & Plantic

reuse plastic bags
don't get any new ones, don't throw them out

banana leaves takeaway food

paper cups are made unrecyclable by a thin layer of interior plastic

get your own reusable coffee cup

enjoy some new plastic alternatives!

review

seaweed pouches bags & packets

fibre compostables meal trays

replace your tyres regularly
93% of microplastics come from tyre dust

replace

wet-wipes

teabags

use plastic-free soap bars
for shampoo & shower gel

use toothpaste tabs
tubes are a recycling nightmare

look out for available substitutes
all these products have established sustainable alternatives

coffee pods

shrink wrap

washable rags
instead of disposable wipes

plates, cutlery

polystyrene foam

size = impact

join or start a plastic-picking club
#trashtag

think circular
gonna keep saying it over & over
▸140

bin your cigarettes
cigarette butts & filters are one of the highest plastic waste products

rethink

watch where that cap or lid is going
10% of all plastic waste

recycle

don't be duped by 'bio-bottles'

double-check 'compostable'

labels can lie: industrially compostable means it must be picked up & treated by your local authority

don't be seduced by 'biodegradable'

beauty & cosmetic packaging
only 50% is recycled

rinse out & wash your plastics before recycling

contaminated waste usually ends up in landfill

plastic bin-liners
wash out & line with newspaper

plastic straws
metal, paper - anything is better

carry your own cutlery
don't use those at cafes & takeouts, etc. They're just dumped afterwards

refuse

saran wrap/ clingfilm
PVC is the worst! Persists for centuries

sachets are the devil!
48% end up dumped. Try to avoid them

avoid food delivery using plastic containers
or petition for returnables if you really like their food!

buy food that isn't over-packaged

sources: New York Times, Guardian, Our World in Data

Blood donors Canada and receive a text when their is used

in Sweden,
the UK

blood

The blood you donated has
now helped a patient! Thanks!

sources: Global News Canada, Independent, NHS

The Death Penalty is Disappearing
Nations who have banned

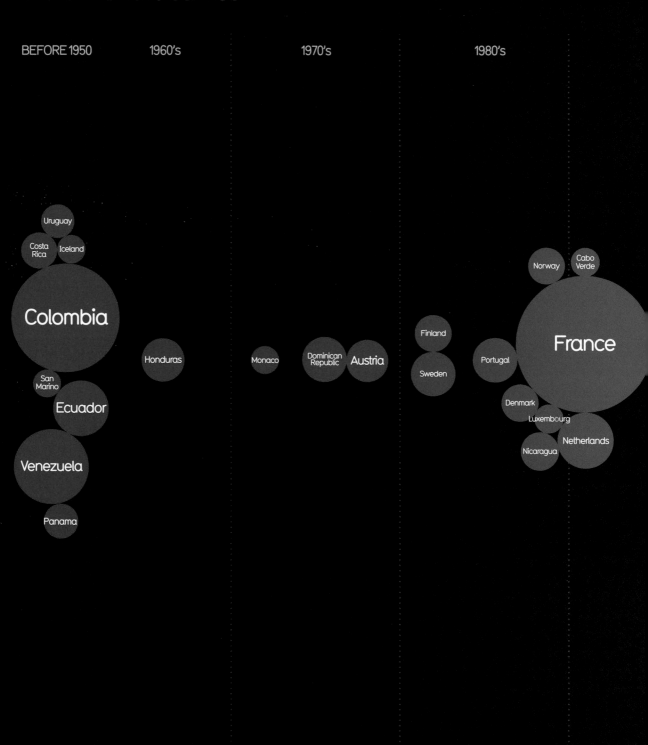

BEFORE 1950   1960's   1970's   1980's

Uruguay

Costa Rica   Iceland

Colombia

Honduras   Monaco   Dominican Republic   Austria

Finland   Cabo Verde
                                                Norway

San Marino   Portugal   France

Ecuador   Sweden

                                                                    Denmark
Venezuela   Luxembourg
                                                                              Netherlands
                                                                    Nicaragua

Panama

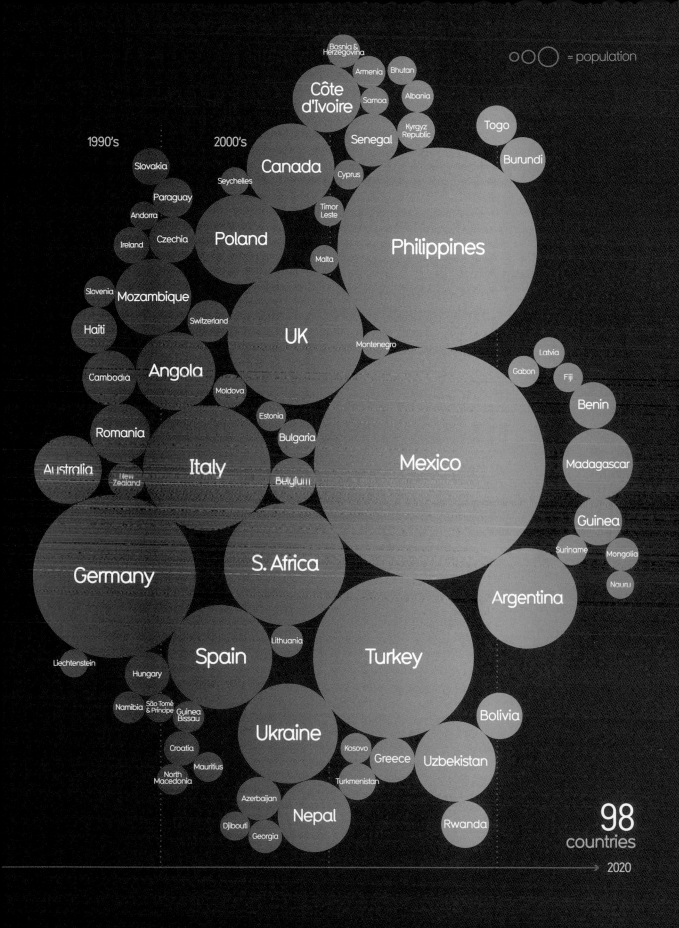

○ ◯ ◯ = population

1990's   2000's

Bosnia &
Herzegovina
Armenia   Bhutan
Côte
d'Ivoire   Samoa   Albania
Slovakia   Kyrgyz   Togo
Senegal   Republic
Seychelles   Canada   Cyprus   Burundi
Paraguay   Timor
Andorra   Leste
Ireland   Czechia   Poland   Malta
Slovenia   Philippines
Mozambique   Switzerland
Haiti   UK   Montenegro
Angola   Latvia
Cambodia   Gabon   Fiji
Moldova   Benin
Romania   Estonia
Bulgaria   Mexico   Madagascar
Australia   Italy
New   Belgium   Guinea
Zealand   Suriname   Mongolia
Germany   S. Africa   Argentina   Nauru
Liechtenstein   Lithuania
Hungary   Spain   Turkey
Namibia   São Tomé   Guinea   Bolivia
& Príncipe   Bissau
Croatia   Kosovo   Uzbekistan
North   Mauritius   Ukraine   Greece
Macedonia   Turkmenistan
Azerbaijan   Rwanda
Djibouti   Nepal
Georgia

98
countries

2020

Unexpectedly Positive Things to Arise out of the Tragedy of the Coronavirus Pandemic

Millions Volunteered...
to help fight the coronavirus on all fronts

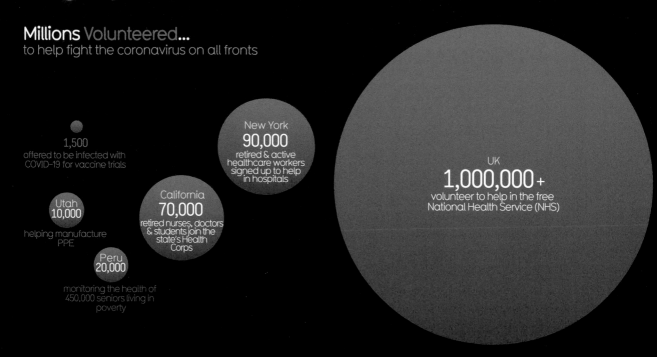

1,500
offered to be infected with
COVID-19 for vaccine trials

Utah
10,000
helping manufacture
PPE

Peru
20,000
monitoring the health of
450,000 seniors living in
poverty

California
70,000
retired nurses, doctors
& students join the
state's Health
Corps

New York
90,000
retired & active
healthcare workers
signed up to help
in hospitals

UK
1,000,000+
volunteer to help in the free
National Health Service (NHS)

sources: Guardian, Scientific American, New York Times, NBC

Cases of Flu Crashed
Number of positive influenza tests per week, N. America

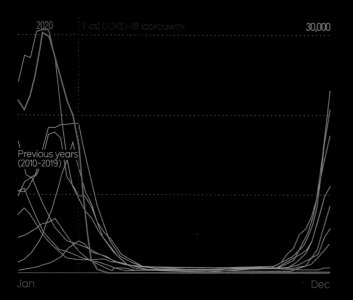

2020

First COVID-19 lockdowns

30,000

Previous years
(2010–2019)

Jan

Dec

source: Scientific American

Emissions from Aviation Dropped
Megatonnes of C02 in 2020 vs 2019

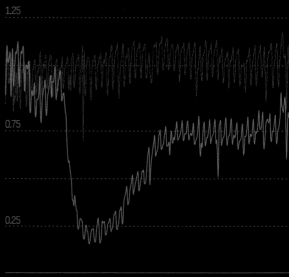

1.25

0.75

0.25

source: US Bureau of Justice Statistics

Lockdown Measures Saved Millions
Minimum lives saved....

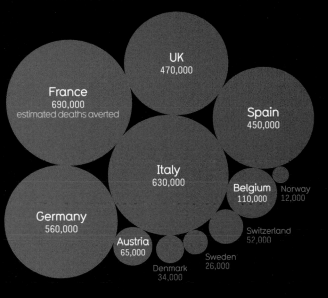

France
690,000
estimated deaths averted

UK
470,000

Spain
450,000

Italy
630,000

Germany
560,000

Belgium
110,000

Norway
12,000

Austria
65,000

Switzerland
52,000

Denmark
34,000

Sweden
26,000

source. Nature (journal)

We've Never Developed Such Powerful & Effective Vaccines So Quickly...

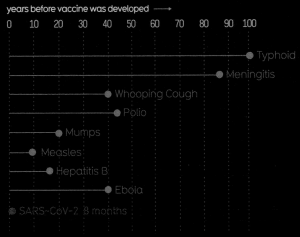

years before vaccine was developed ⟶

0 10 20 30 40 50 60 70 80 90 100

Typhoid
Meningitis
Whooping Cough
Polio
Mumps
Measles
Hepatitis B
Ebola
SARS-CoV-2 8 months

Thanks to unprecendented international funding,
resources, collaboration and sharing of research

source: Nature (journal)

Traffic Congestion Plummeted
Hours stuck in traffic per average driver per year

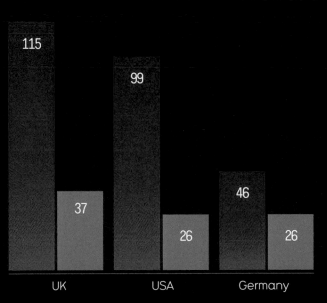

115
37
99
26
46
26

UK   USA   Germany

sources: Centers for Disease Control, Pew Research Center

We can recycle our plastic disposable face masks into roads to reduce waste

1 km of road would use up 3 million masks,
preventing 93 tonnes of waste going to landfill.

6.8 billion masks are used worldwide daily.
That's 2,268 km of potential road surface.

sources: Centers for Disease Control, Pew Research Center

Corporate Power Pledges

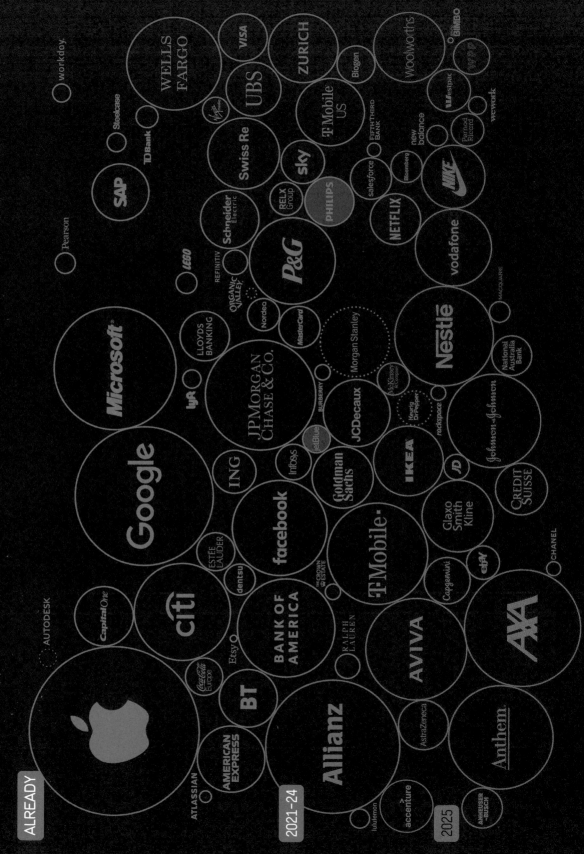

size = revenue

100% renewable electricity

100% renewable energy

carbon neutral/ zero

ALREADY

2021-24

2025

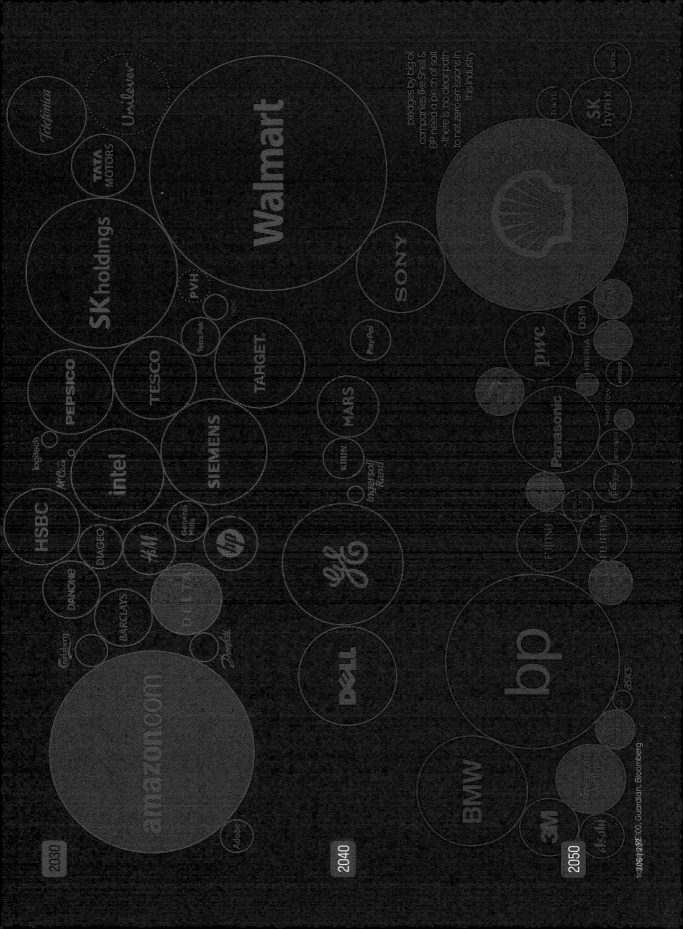

2030

Telefónica

Unilever

TATA MOTORS

SKholdings

Walmart

PEPSICO

TESCO

PVH

next.

Tetra Pak

SIEMENS

TARGET

SONY

logitech

WR.Grace

intel

SK hynix

Esmée

bavi

pledges by big oil
companies like Shell &
BP need a pinch of salt
– there is no clear path
to net zero emissions in
this industry

HSBC

DIAGEO

4M

General Mills

HP

PayPal

MARS

KIRIN

Ingersoll Rand

DSM

IBERIA

pwc

milton

DANONE

BARCLAYS

DELTA

Danfoss

Carlsberg

amazon.com

Adobe

2040

GE

DELL

Panasonic

Heathrow

Kellogg

FUJITSU

FUJIFILM

2050

BMW

bp

3M

ASICS

3M

Ariston

s2061-20FE100, Guardian, Bloomberg

City & Country Climate Pledges

REGION
STATE
city

IMPACT (population)

IMPLIED (not pledged)

TRANSITION	% RENEWABLE ENERGY	REDUCTION	ELIMINATION
% RENEWABLE ELECTRICITY ▲ 100%		% DECREASE EMISSIONS / GHGs	NET ZERO / CARBON NEUTRAL

now
Helsinki
KENYA
Melbourne

2025
Adelaide
BRAZIL
Copenhagen
NEW ZEALAND
PUERTO RICO
San Francisco

2030
Amsterdam
AUSTRALIA
Boulder
BRAZIL
CHINA
DENMARK
EUROPEAN UNION
Glasgow
Hamburg
LATIN AMERICA
Nevada
New York City
NORWAY
Oslo
San Francisco
Sydney
UK
Washington DC
Helsinki
NEW ZEALAND

2040
New York
PUERTO RICO
Stockholm

2045
CALIFORNIA
Glasgow
HAWAII
Los Angeles
NEW MEXICO
SWEDEN
WASHINGTON

2050
Amsterdam
Boulder
Chicago
DENMARK
EUROPEAN UNION
FINLAND
FRANCE
Hamburg
JAPAN
London
Los Angeles
Minneapolis
Nevada
New York City
NEW ZEALAND
Portland
Puerto Rico
Rio de Janeiro
San Francisco
Seattle
SOUTH KOREA
SWEDEN
Sydney
Toronto
USA
Vancouver
Washington DC
Yokohoma

2060
BRAZIL
CHINA

phase out fossil fuels

fossil-fuel free

sources Carbon Neutral Cities Alliances, Reuters, New York Times, WWF, Guardian, Climate Action Tracker

Things Going Down! Down! Down!
in a good way

Discriminatory Policies
against ethnic minorities

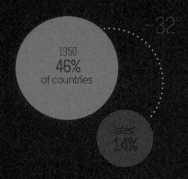

~32%

1950
46%
of countries

latest
14%

Global Death Penalty
executions per year

~62%

11.4k

4.4k

1990   2016

Hours of Housework
average weekly hours

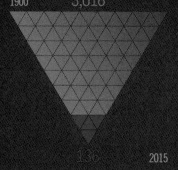

1900   3,016

136   2015

Lab-Grown Meat
cost per pound

$500,000

$363

2013   2020

Child Labour
% of children 5-17 in work

Year	Value
1950	27.5
1960	
1970	
1980	
1990	
1995	13
2000	16
2004	
2008	
2012	10.5
2016	9.5

different data sources used

Stunted Growth
kids under 5

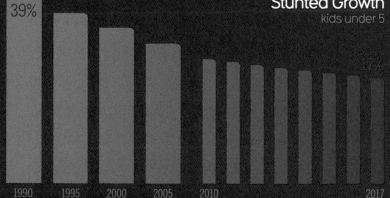

39%

17%

1990   1995   2000   2005   2010   2017

sources: World Bank, The Economist, Cato Institute, University of Maryland, Our World in Data

Land Preservation **Is Happening**

PROTECTED AREA
square kilometres

972
Northeast Greenland Park
World's largest national park
& land protection area

924
Nigeria

EQUIVALENT SIZE

A global agreement
to restore the
world's deforested
& degraded land.
2030 target:
3.5 million
square kilometres

1,727
The Bonn Challenge

1,648
Iran

72.4
Mexico

80
D.R.Congo

120
Brazil

150
USA

210
India

150
Ethiopia

120
Cameroon

70
Ireland

147
Nepal

79
Czechnia

213
Kansas

120
North Korea

120
Pennsylvania

safeguards
biodiversity

increases
CO2 absorption

ensures clean
air & water

adds resilience
to natural disasters

54 countries have
signed up

The Great Bear
Rainforest
British Columbia,
Canada

158

Canada signed
deals with First
Nations people,
timber companies
and environmental
organisations to
protects its forests

147

AREA THE
SIZE OF
Bangladesh

Birch River Park
Alberta, Canada

67

70

Ireland

Cosmic Village of
the Jaguars
Colombia

43

Serranía de
Chiribiquete is the
biggest protected
tropical rainforest
park in the world

43

Denmark

Lake Titicaca
Peru & Bolivia

8.4

$500m deal to
preserve the largest
lake in S. America

9.2

Cyprus

Tompkins Conservation
Chile & Argentina

8

American foundation
has bought & donated
national park land

9.1

Puerto Rico

sources: BBC, Bonn Challenge, National Geographic

Protecting the Surface of the Earth

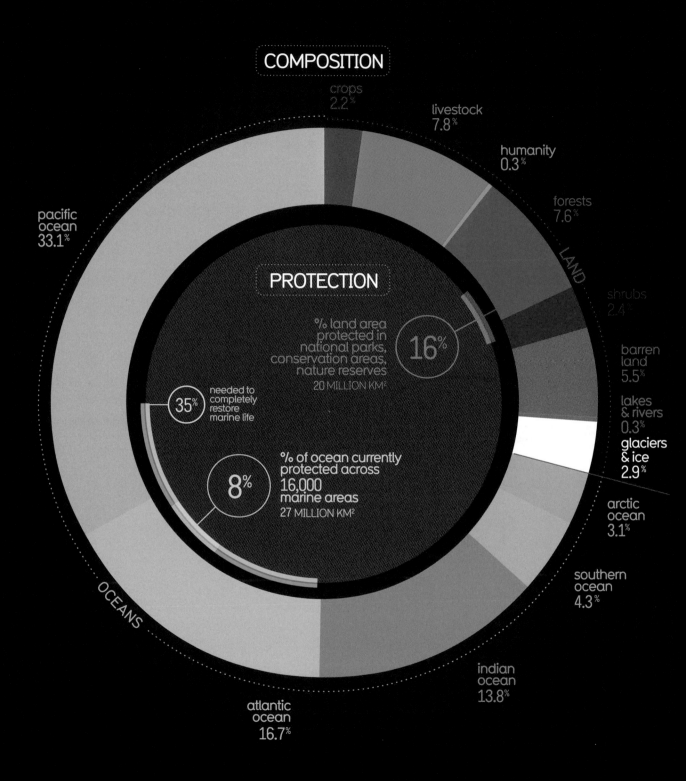

COMPOSITION

crops
2.2%

livestock
7.8%

humanity
0.3%

forests
7.6%

LAND

shrubs
2.4%

barren
land
5.5%

lakes
& rivers
0.3%

glaciers
& ice
2.9%

arctic
ocean
3.1%

southern
ocean
4.3%

indian
ocean
13.8%

atlantic
ocean
16.7%

OCEANS

pacific
ocean
33.1%

PROTECTION

% land area
protected in
national parks,
conservation areas,
nature reserves
20 MILLION KM²

16%

35% needed to
completely
restore
marine life

8% % of ocean currently
protected across
16,000
marine areas
27 MILLION KM²

sources: Our World in Data, Wikipedia,

LED Bulbs

Use Far Less Energy to Generate the Same Amount of Light...

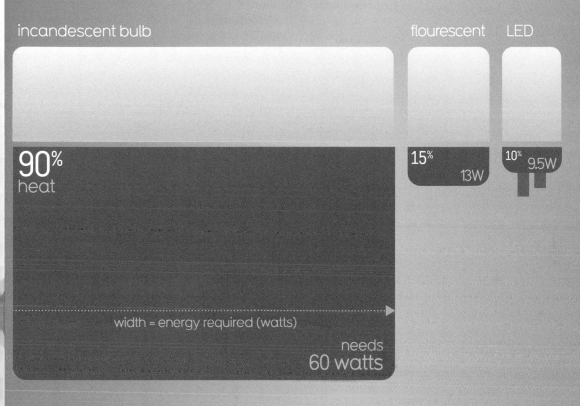

incandescent bulb

flourescent   LED

90%
heat

15%
13W

10%   9.5W

width = energy required (watts)

needs
60 watts

...Saving Energy & Money

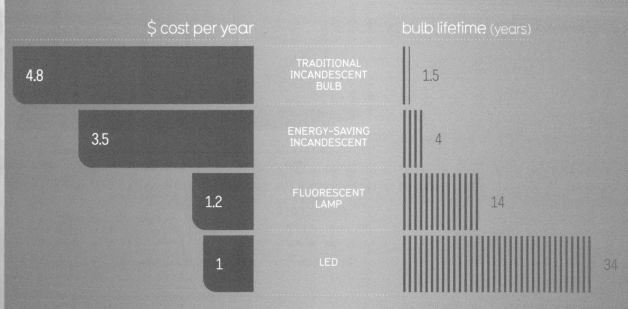

$ cost per year

bulb lifetime (years)

4.8   TRADITIONAL INCANDESCENT BULB   1.5

3.5   ENERGY-SAVING INCANDESCENT   4

1.2   FLUORESCENT LAMP   14

1   LED   34

sources: International Energy Agency, energy.gov

Is it Wrong to Fly?

From nearly 100,000 daily flights in a typical year

45,000 just in the USA

But closer to 5–8% of climate impact due to high-altitude release of gases & vapours

CARBON DIOXIDE

NITROUS OXIDE

SOOT .... plays a key role in contrails, which increase warming

WATER VAPOUR

relative global heating effects (radiative forcing) of major components of aviation emissions

Air travel accounts for ~2.5% of global greenhouse gas emissions

It's definitely one of the worst forms of transport, emissions-wise

GRAMS OF CO2 PER PASSENGER KILOMETRE

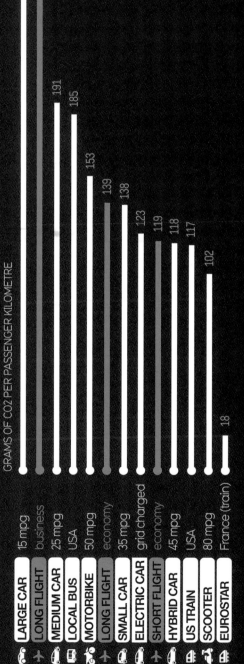

		grams CO2
LARGE CAR	15 mpg	312
LONG FLIGHT	business	297
MEDIUM CAR	25 mpg	191
LOCAL BUS	USA	185
MOTORBIKE	50 mpg	153
LONG FLIGHT	economy	139
SMALL CAR	35 mpg	138
ELECTRIC CAR	grid charged	123
SHORT FLIGHT	economy	119
HYBRID CAR	45 mpg	118
US TRAIN	USA	117
SCOOTER	80 mpg	102
EUROSTAR	France (train)	18

Flying has become an essential part of our society, culture & economy

MILLIONS OF FLIGHTS PER YEAR

...It's not going away

And nor are its emissions

PREDICTED INCREASE

between

240%

and

360%

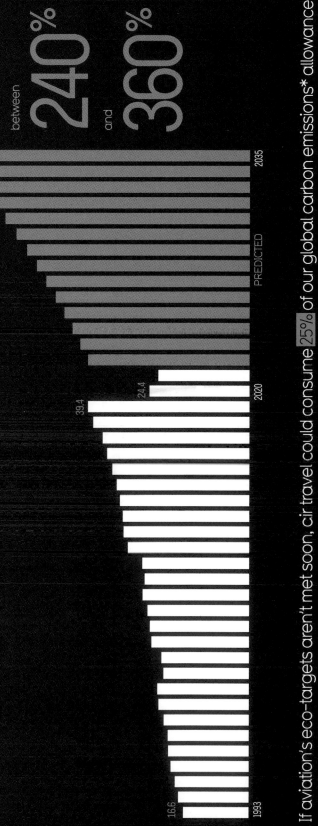

71.6

39.4

24.4

16.6

1993

2020

2035

PREDICTED

If aviation's eco-targets aren't met soon, air travel could consume 25% of our global carbon emissions* allowance

12.5% if 50% CO2-emission-reduction targets are met

Paris Agreement carbon budget to stay under 1.5°C

* Paris Agreement carbon budget to stay under 1.5°C

But if everyone just stopped flying, it would have a minor impact on emissions

And many things are as bad or worse emitters & maybe easier to tackle...

AIR TRAVE...

SHIPPING

FOOD WASTE
▶162

LANDFILLS

CARS
▶141

Sources: New York Times, Carbon Brief, IPCC, National Geographic, NRDC, IATA

Some Solutions Are Ready for Take-Off

Global agreement where airlines commit to using sustainable aerofuels or offsets to cancel out emissions from international flights

192 countries onboard

non-mandatory until 2027

not domestic flights
Paris Agreement covers those

private jets exempt

Sustainable Aerofuels

 Up to 80% emissions savings across entire lifecycle

 Not here yet – still expensive & difficult to produce

 Stringent safety requirements means uptake is low

 Will work best for international flights (400 miles or more)

Boosting Aircraft Efficiency

% IMPROVEMENT SINCE 1980

+1–2% PER YEAR

162

112

67

33

Lighter materials, next-gen engines

27% LESS FUEL BURNED

15% WEIGHT REDUCTION

New aerodynamic plane designs

Better Personal Choices

THE 12% OF US ADULTS WHO TAKE 6+ FLIGHTS A YEAR
ARE RESPONSIBLE FOR 70% OF ALL US AVIATION EMISSIONS

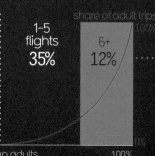

those taking zero flights **53%**

1–5 flights **35%**

6+ **12%**

share of adult trips
100%

0%

0%   % of American adults   100%

 choose direct flights
they're better because 25% of emissions occur on take-off and landing

 consider cabin class
first-class passengers use 5x the emissions of economy by taking up more plane space

reduce unnecessary flights

 seek alternative transport
trains, especially electric trains in Europe, are most ideal – but US trains are fossil-fuel powered

offset your flight emissions
there are some good schemes – see our guide 220

sources: US Bureau of Transport, Nat Geo, World Bank

Electric Planes?

Top Speed km/h

Boeing 747	965
Airbus A320	904
Cessna*	800
Helicopter	300
Alice	440

$Fuel Cost per 100km

400
207
100
42
6

Passenger Capacity

Cessna	8
Alice	9
Heli	18
A320	150
747	660

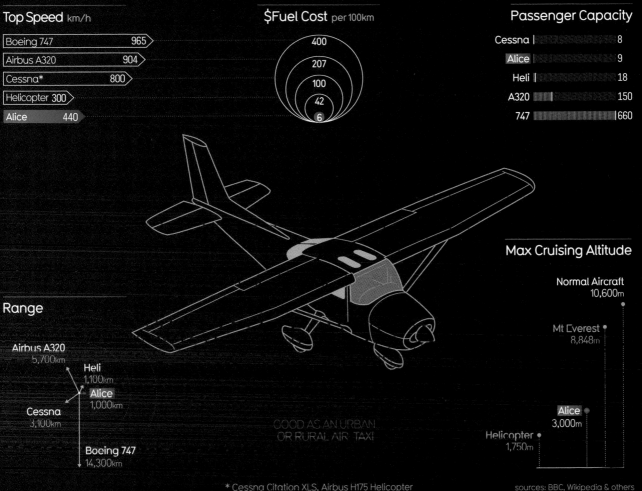

GOOD AS AN URBAN
OR RURAL AIR TAXI

Range

Airbus A320
5,700km

Heli
1,100km

Alice
1,000km

Cessna
3,100km

Boeing 747
14,300km

Max Cruising Altitude

Normal Aircraft
10,600m

Mt Everest
8,848m

Alice
3,000m

Helicopter
1,750m

* Cessna Citation XLS, Airbus H175 Helicopter

sources: BBC, Wikipedia & others

Challenges

OVER 200 ELECTRIC PLANE DESIGNS ARE IN DEVELOPMENT BUT THE TECHNOLOGICAL HURDLES ARE HIGH

The aviation industry is built on energy-dense fuels	An electric 747 would need a battery	Future battery tech might reduce this	Hydrogen or hybrid-electric planes are possible

Gasoline is incredibly energy dense	7x heavier than the plane itself	But by not nearly enough	But continued use of aerofuels more likely at least for international flights

sources: BBC, Wikipedia

Does Carbon Offsetting Really Work?

when you reduce emissions in one place to compensate for emissions you caused somewhere else

 so to offset the 1.5 tonnes of CO2 on your transatlantic return flight

you might invest in programmes to support

renewable energy

clean-water access

cleaner cookstoves

tree planting

problem!

there are no global or national regulations in most countries on what a carbon offset is

so anyone can sell one

early programmes proved useless, even fraudulent

but today, some beautiful news

Gold Standard ········ solid independent certifications exist ········ **Green-e**

what makes a good one?

high quality schemes need to be

real	verified	enforceable	permanent	additional	leak-proof
the project actually exists	independent 3rd-party checks	repercussions if not completed	not easily reversible	accomplishing something new	emissions stopped not just shifted

ultimately, do offsets work?

mathematically	socially/politically	ethically
\nYES	\nKINDA	\nUNCLEAR
If executed well, and are high quality, they can deliver a fair offset	Does voluntary offsetting take the pressure off corporate polluters & detract from systemic issues?	Is it okay for people in rich countries to just 'buy out' their climate guilt ?

sources: IPCC, National Geographic, Natural Resources Defence Council

50 Countries Have Reduced Their Overuse of Fertilisers

Decrease in nitrogen, potash & phosphate per hectare

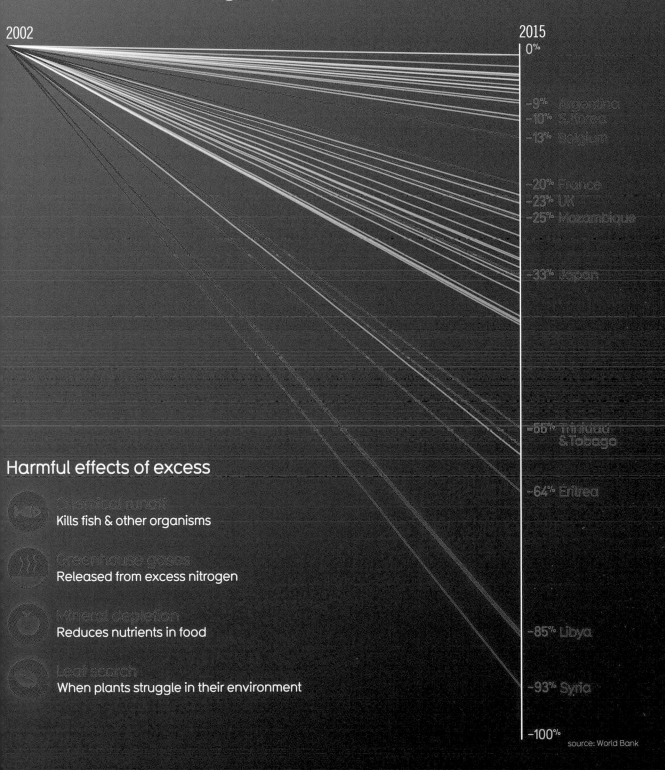

2002

2015

0%

-9% Argentina
-10% S.Korea
-13% Belgium

-20% France
-23% UK
-25% Mozambique

-33% Japan

-55% Trinidad &Tobago

-64% Eritrea

-85% Libya

-93% Syria

-100%

source: World Bank

Harmful effects of excess

Chemical runoff
Kills fish & other organisms

Greenhouse gases
Released from excess nitrogen

Mineral depletion
Reduces nutrients in food

Leaf scorch
When plants struggle in their environment

More than
institutions
have de-ir
$14 TRILLIO
from fossil-
companie

1,200

worldwide

vested

fuel

breakdown of institutions

faith institutions 15% de-invested		philanthropy 17%
education 15%		pension funds 14%
government 15%	corporations 6%	
	NGOs 4%	health care 1%

source: GoFossilFree.org

The Potential of Hydrogen Power Is Amazing!

true natural resource
super-abundant, non-toxic element – will never run out

no direct emissions
burns cleanly – releasing only energy & water

highly stable
can be liquified & stored in fuel cells for weeks & years

easy to transport
via pipelines, or in trucks and ships

H is already in use around the world – and its potential looks rosy
size = potential

ALREADY	DEFINITELY	PROBABLY	PROBLEMATIC
done deal	**makes sense**	**some obstacles**	**major issues**
rocket fuel	air-taxis	trucks/lorries	buses
oil refining	domestic heating	short-haul flights	shipping
making fertiliser	steel production	industrial transport	long-haul flights
first fuel-cell cars	industrial heating		widespread cars
	energy storage		

main problem

It's currently difficult to manufacture **H** without emitting carbon

TYPE OF HYDROGEN	GREY	BLUE	BLACK/BROWN	YELLOW	GREEN
WHAT	made from fossil fuels, mostly methane	same as grey but CO2 is captured	made with types of coal	synthesised with nuclear energy	renewable energy to extract **H** from water
% OF CURRENT GLOBAL H	76	0	23	0	2
$ PER KILO	$1-3	$1.5 ideal price	$2	unknown	$2.5-6
NOTE	every tonne of H generates 11 tonnes of CO2	not here yet, CO2 capture tech in its infancy ▸214	dirty tech – needs to be phased out	strong possibility for carbon-free hydrogen	

versatile
can be 'dropped in' existing
natural gas grid & boilers

a decent bet
could supply up to 20% of
global emissions – free energy

high energy density
more energy per kilogram
than most fuels, inc. gasoline

better than batteries
in terms of power-to-weight,
but not in efficiency

Global Production Is Ramping Up
With big plans for the future

18 million tonnes H produced per year

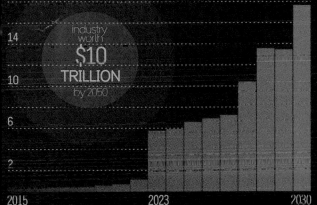

industry worth **$10 TRILLION** by 2050

14

10

6

2

2015   2023   2030

	Hydrogen Fuel Cell	Lithium Battery	Petrol/ Gasoline
energy density kilowatt hours per kilo	34	0.3	13
efficiency % energy in to energy out	38%	80%	25%
mass required kg for a 300km car journey	5	540	40

Major Players Have Entered the Race

European Union
€470bn
investment
by 2050

Russia
not going to
be left behind

UK building a
'world-leading'
blue H plant

**ermany, Portugal,
Netherlands**
leading in Europe

China
already world's
largest producer

South America
Brazil & Argentina
all potential green
H exporters

Japan
plans to build first
'hydrogen society'

Saudi Arabia
aims to transition
to H economy

Challenges Ahead Though

leaky
hydrogen
molecules

flammable
& highly
explosive

new safety
standards &
infrastructure
required

manufacturing
has got to use
low-carbon electricity
– or else there's
no point

current green
electrolysis
is very costly

sources: Carbon Brief, International Energy Agency, 'How to Avoid a Climate Disaster' (Gates, 2020)

What about H-Fuelled Passenger Cars?
Are Fuel Cell Electric Vehicles (FCEVs) a true alternative to 'battery electric'?

fuel-celled
electricity generated from onboard supply of H tanks

fast refuelling
can fill up at a traditional gas station in 5 mins

refuelling network
infrastructure will need to be built

industial storage
expensive level of gas compression required

Overall Efficiency Is Less Than Electric
% OF ENERGY DELIVERED TO WHEELS

| 16 | 30 | 33 | 49 | 77 | 88 |
| gasoline | | hydrogen | | electric | |

But Max Range Is About the Same
MILES BEFORE RECHARGE

- BMW X5 — H
- VOLKSWAGEN ID 3
- TESLA MODEL X
- HYUNDAI NEXO — H
- TOYOTA MIRA — H
- TESLA MODEL S

they're off!
About 9,000 FCEVs on already on Californian roads

520

200

402
380
360
336

Big Car Makers Are Split
MANY ARE ALREADY WEDDED TO BATTERIES

OUT

Audi
FIAT   DAIMLER Mercedes-Benz
Volkswagen
TESLA
General Motors

IN

HYUNDAI
HONDA
BMW
TOYOTA

Ford   ON THE FENCE   NISSAN

H vans & lorries
most manufacturers are investing in H-powered fuel cell trucks for commercial fleets

ultimately H needs to be green & carbon-free
only H produced from renewable energy like solar & wind makes sense
or else we're just adding more emissions

Hydrogen Aircraft Could be Possible
But at least 10 years away

planes will have to be redesigned to accomodate fuel cells

liquified hydrogen needs 4x the storage of kerosene airfuels

long haul unlikely
Compounding effect of greater storage, aircraft design, etc. makes hydrogen long haul very challenging

short & medium haul is feasible
The EU is shooting for 2035-2040 for hydrogen-powered flights of less than four hours (which cause 60% of aviation's emissions)

fuel cell air-taxis
Like a big drone, basically, but powered by lighter hydrogen fuel cells for increased lift and range - 5 people up to 600 km.

hybrids possible
Using H in flight to power fuel cells, or combining with CO_2 to create new synthetic liquid fuels, may mean less change to existing infrastructure

---

A Hydrogen PowerPaste for Scooters, Motorcycles & Drones
Amazing new solution for small vehicles

H is combined with magnesium to make powdered magnesium hydride

adding water activates a chemical reaction to produce H to drive a motor

10x energy density of electric battery

functional from ~30 to 250 degrees C

stored in swappable cartridges & cannisters

sources: Fraunhofer Institute, Airbus, Carbon Brief, The Week, 'How to Avoid a Climate Disaster' (Bill Gates, 2020)

Protests Engaging 3.5% of a Population Very Rarely Fail

Major movements 1960 onwards

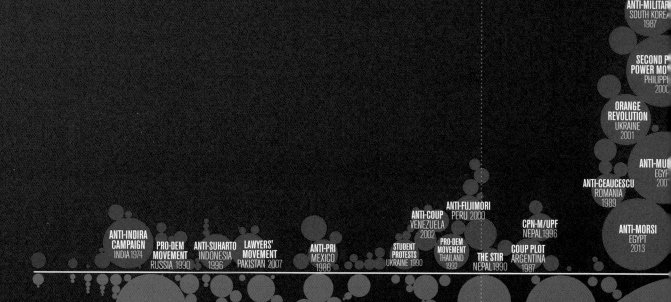

ANTI-MILITAR
SOUTH KORE
1987

SECOND P
POWER MO
PHILIPPI
2000

ORANGE
REVOLUTION
UKRAINE
2001

ANTI-MU
EGYP
200

ANTI-CEAUCESCU
ROMANIA
1989

ANTI-FUJIMORI
PERU 2000

ANTI-COUP
VENEZUELA
2002

CPN-M/UPF
NEPAL 1996

ANTI-MORSI
EGYPT
2013

ANTI-INDIRA
CAMPAIGN
INDIA 1974

PRO-DEM
MOVEMENT
RUSSIA 1990

ANTI-SUHARTO
INDONESIA
1996

LAWYERS'
MOVEMENT
PAKISTAN 2007

ANTI-PRI
MEXICO
1986

STUDENT
PROTESTS
UKRAINE 1990

PRO-DEM
MOVEMENT
THAILAND
1992

THE STIR
NEPAL 1990

COUP PLOT
ARGENTINA
1987

FAILED

0.1% OF POPULATION ENGAGED (LOG)

1%

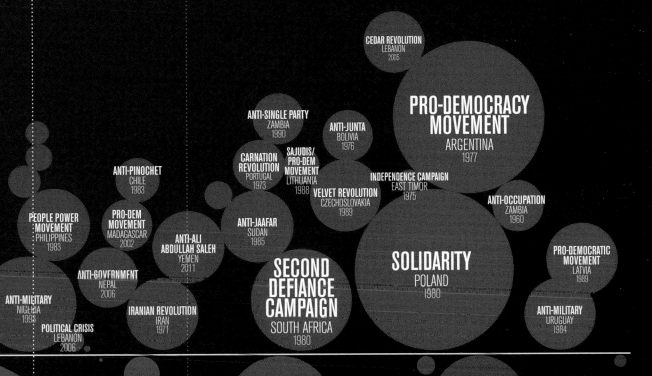

3.5%

CEDAR REVOLUTION
LEBANON
2005

PRO-DEMOCRACY
MOVEMENT
ARGENTINA
1977

ANTI-SINGLE PARTY
ZAMBIA
1990

ANTI-JUNTA
BOLIVIA
1976

CARNATION
REVOLUTION
PORTUGAL
1973

SAJUDIS/
PRO-DEM
MOVEMENT
LITHUANIA
1988

INDEPENDENCE CAMPAIGN
EAST TIMOR
1975

ANTI-PINOCHET
CHILE
1983

VELVET REVOLUTION
CZECHOSLOVAKIA
1989

ANTI-OCCUPATION
ZAMBIA
1960

PEOPLE POWER
MOVEMENT
PHILIPPINES
1983

PRO-DEM
MOVEMENT
MADAGASCAR
2002

ANTI-JAAFAR
SUDAN
1985

SOLIDARITY
POLAND
1980

PRO-DEMOCRATIC
MOVEMENT
LATVIA
1989

ANTI-ALI
ABDULLAH SALEH
YEMEN
2011

SECOND
DEFIANCE
CAMPAIGN
SOUTH AFRICA
1980

ANTI-GOVERNMENT
NEPAL
2006

ANTI-MILITARY
URUGUAY
1984

ANTI-MILITARY
NIGERIA
1998

IRANIAN REVOLUTION
IRAN
1971

POLITICAL CRISIS
LEBANON
2006

 = no. of protestors

3.5%

10%

100%

source: Nonviolent & Violent Campaigns and Outcomes (NAVCO) Data Project

REF
REDUC
REUSE
REPAIR
REPURPOSE
RECYCLE
(last resort)

USE
E

Armies Everywhere Are Shrinking
Soldiers as % of population

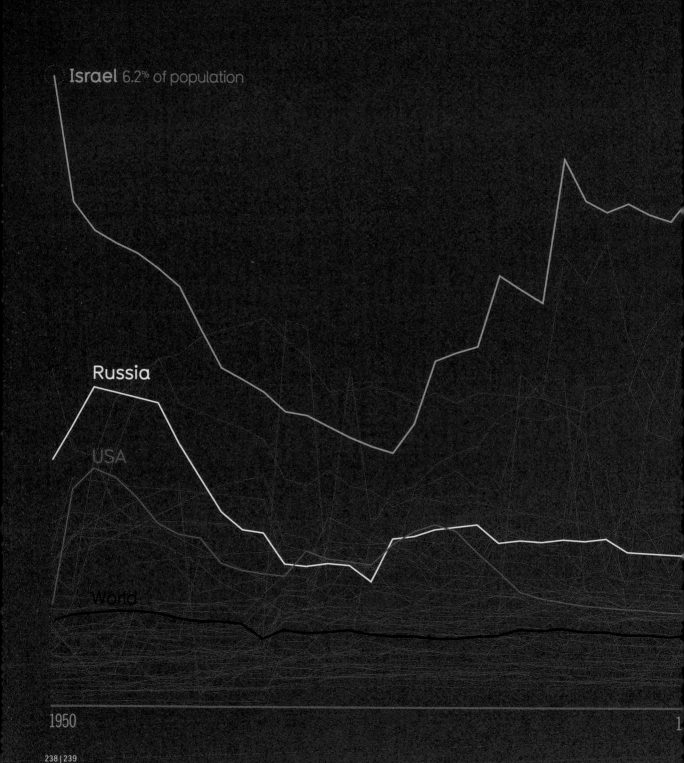

Israel 6.2% of population

Russia

USA

World

1950

Iraq 7.7%

N. Korea 4.8%

2012

Source: Our World in Data

Famine Deaths Have Plummeted Globally

1960s
5,470 DEATHS per million people

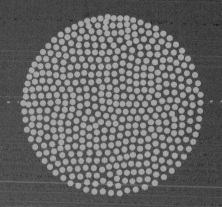

2000s
460

2010-2016
40

source: Our World in Data

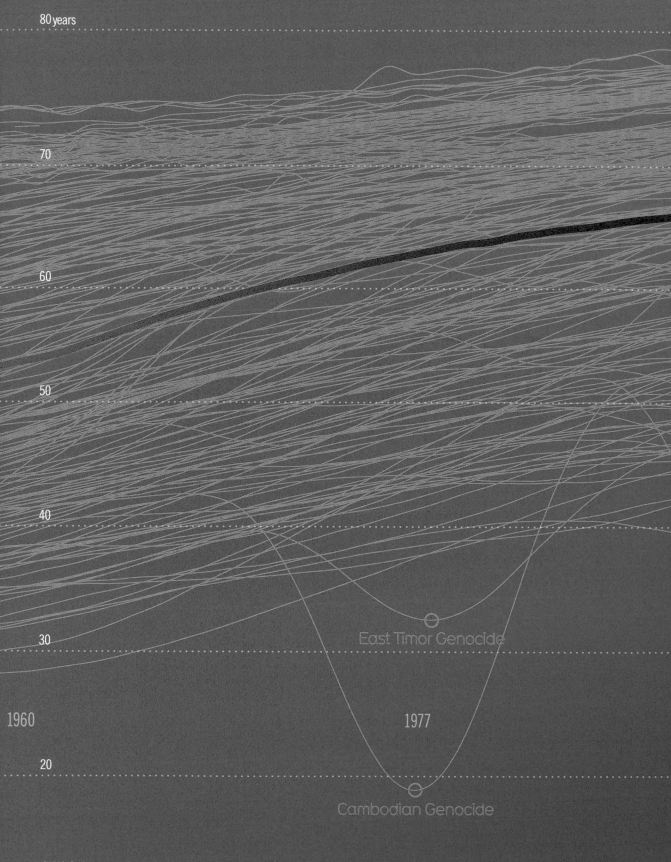

80 years

70

60

50

40

30

East Timor Genocide

1960

1977

20

Cambodian Genocide

AVERAGE: 72

AIDS epidemic in
Sub-Saharan Africa

Sierra Leone
Civil War

1993 Rwandan Genocide

2018

Everyone, Everywhere Is Living Longer
Average life expectancy in each country

sources: GapMinder, Our World in Data

Because Every Country Is Most Beautiful at Something

MOST LGBTQ+ FRIENDLY
Sweden

MOST ELECTRIC CARS
Norway

MOST INCLUSIVE
Finland

BOX OFFICE HIT PRODUCTION
Canada

SAFEST COUNTRY
Iceland

FREEDOM OF EXPRESSION
Denmark

ONLINE USER RIGHTS
Estonia

FREE SANITARY PRODUCTS
Scotland

MOST WOMEN
Latvia

OFFSHORE WIND
UK

BIOGAS
Germany

FEWEST KIDNAPPINGS
Lithuania

MOST GENEROUS DONORS TO CHARITY
USA

FLOWERS!
Netherlands

FIRST BLOND BEER
Cze. Rep.

CRYPTOCURRENCY
Belarus

GDP GROWTH
Ireland

FEWEST MOTHERS DYING
Poland

ENVIRONMENTAL QUALITY
France

INVENTED POSTCARDS
Austria

JUSTICE
Italy

CHEAPEST BROADBAND
Ukraine

STRAWBERRIES
Mexico

CONCENTRATED SOLAR POWER
Spain

APPLE EXPOR
Moldova

MOST DOCTORS
Cuba

SAFEST ROADS
Switzerland

LOWEST MALE CANCER
Romania

FIRST MODERN BLACK REPUBLIC
Haiti

INCOME EQUALITY
Slovenia

LOWEST FEMALE CA
Bu

FIRST STOCK EXCHANGE
Jamaica

CHILDREN'S RIGHTS
Portugal

CARDAMONS
Guatemala

FEWEST SMOKERS
Honduras

ORGANIC BANANAS
Dominican Rep.

KIDNEY TRANSPLANTS
Croatia

TOP TRAVEL DESTINAT
Gre

FIRST TO BAN METAL MINING
El Salvador

LEAST ILLEGAL CIGARETTES
Nicaragua

FIRST DOLPHIN CAPTIVITY BANS
Hungary

LEAST SLUMS
Costa Rica

MOST PROTECTED LAND AREA
Venezuela

MOST IMPROVED DEMOCRACY
Albania

BEST FOREST PROTECTIONS
Panama

MOST FORESTS
Suriname

FOREIGN INVESTMENT
Serbia

NATURE RIGHTS
Ecuador

MOST BIRD SPECIES
Colombia

LOWEST METHANE EMISSIONS
Kosovo

BEST CUISINE
Peru

MOST PLANTS
Brazil

FIRST FULL WIRELESS BROADBAND
North Macedonia

MOST SUSTAINABLE FORESTS
Bolivia

HYDROPOWER
Paraguay

BEST FOR GREEN TOURISM
Chile

MOST PETS
Argentina

COOL TECH

DEVELOPMENT

FREEDOM & RIGHTS

RENEWABLES

SAFETY

EARLIEST CHRISTIAN STATE
Azerbaijan

MOST KIDS COMPLETING SECONDARY SCHOOL
Kazakhstan

DROP IN TEEN PREGNANCIES
Afghanistan

LOWEST DISEASE DEATH RATE
Japan

LARGEST CONCENTRATED SOLAR POWER PLANT
Morocco

CHESS GRANDMASTERS
Armenia

BEST SOCIAL SAFETY NET
Mongolia

CONTACTLESS PAYMENTS
Georgia

SOLAR PANELS
China

TIDAL POWER
South Korea

IMPROVING COMPETITIVENESS
Cyprus

TEA CONSUMPTION
Turkey

FIRST TO RECOGNISE PALESTINE
Algeria

BIGGEST RISE IN GIRLS ATTENDING SCHOOL
Nepal

MOST STARTUPS
Israel

IMPROVING UNIVERSITIES
Iran

FIRST CARBON-NEGATIVE NATION
Bhutan

FASTEST INTERNET
Taiwan

FEWEST CAR THEFTS
Senegal

INCREASING INTERNET USERS
Iraq

IMPROVING EASE OF BUSINESS
Saudi Arabia

BEST HEALTHCARE
Hong Kong

FEWEST DRINKERS
Mauritania

CAMEL RACERS
Chad

LOWEST UNEMPLOYMENT
Qatar

FIRST TO BAN PLASTIC BAGS
Bangladesh

BEST DIVING
Philippines

TACKLING MALNUTRITION
Mali

ENTIRE COASTLINE PROTECTED
Eritrea

BIGGEST INCREASE IN VEGETABLE INTAKE
Laos

LOWEST DIABETES PREVALENCE
Benin

MOST GENEROUS
Myanmar

LOWEST UNEMPLOYMENT
Cambodia

OUNG PEOPLE
Niger

SCRABBLE PLAYERS
Nigeria

IMPROVING HEALTHCARE ACCESS
Sudan

CASHEWS
Vietnam

NATURAL RUBBER
Thailand

CONTRACEPTIVE ACCESS
Liberia

'KAIZEN'*
Ethiopia

IMPROVING SOCIOECONOMIC EQUALITY

FIRST BIOMETRIC PASSPORT
Malaysia

FASTEST-GROWING ECONOMY
Ghana

Somalia

T CHOCOLATE
Cote d'Ivoire

BEST PEPPERCORNS
Cameroon

BEST RUNNERS
Kenya

MOST GENEROUS VOLUNTEERS
Sri Lanka

FITNESS
Uganda

ROVING PEDESTRIAN SAFETY
Equatorial Guinea

COBALT
Congo

IMPROVING SANITATION
South Sudan

LIFE EXPECTANCY
Singapore

NE GOVERNMENT PARTICIPATION
Gabon

MOST WOMEN MPs
Rwanda

BIGGEST REFORESTATION PROJECT
India

100% RENEWABLE ENERGY
Congo Dem. Rep.

LOWEST CO2 EMISSIONS
Burundi

MOST MAMMALS
Indonesia

BIGGEST DROP IN HUNGER
Angola

FIRST TO VACCINATE AGAINST MALARIA
Malawi

MOST LANGUAGES
Papua New Guinea

PROTECTION OF SEXUAL ORIENTATIONS
Botswana

VANILLA
Madagascar

CONSTITUTIONAL ECO-PROTECTION
Namibia

BIGGEST IMPROVEMENT IN BASIC MEDICAL CARE
Eswatini

MOST NATURAL PARKS
Australia

EDUCATION SPENDING
Lesotho

AVERTED MOST HIV INFECTIONS
South Africa

LEAST CORRUPTION
New Zealand

HEALTH   MONEY   NATURE   NICE!

SKILLZ   WOMEN & GIRLS

sources: so many
* 'kaizen' = Japanese principle of continuous improvement in business

More

In

- explo
- acce
- get
- find

V

- see
- pla

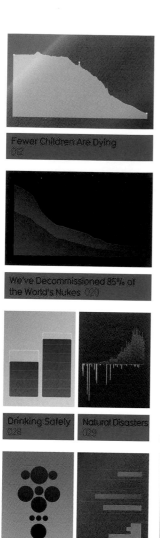

Fewer Children Are Dying
012

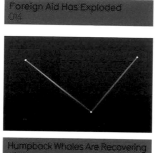

Foreign Aid Has Exploded
014

Women Can Finally Vote Everywhere
016

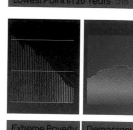

World Hunger Has Reached Its
Lowest Point In 20 Years 018

We've Decommissioned 85% of
the World's Nukes 020

Humpback Whales Are Recovering
022

Solar Panels
024

Extreme Poverty
026

Democracy
027

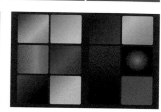

Drinking Safely
028

Natural Disasters
029

Cancer
030

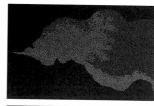

Compilation 1
032

Compilation 2
034

11 Diseases
036

Quick Quiz
037

Answers-Donating-Fake News-
Fossil Fuel Bans 038

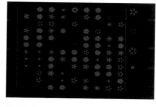

We're Saving Children's Lives
040

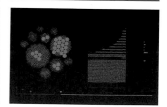

More Girls Are In School
046

Up, up, up
048

Happiness
049

Global Flavours of Contentment
052

Transgender Rights Are Spreading
054

Vaccines!
056

Indigenous
Guardians 058

Creative Ways to Deal With Our
Emissions 060

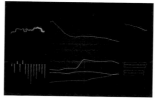

Yay UK!
062

Women
064

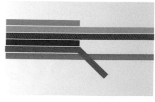

Nuclear Power
066

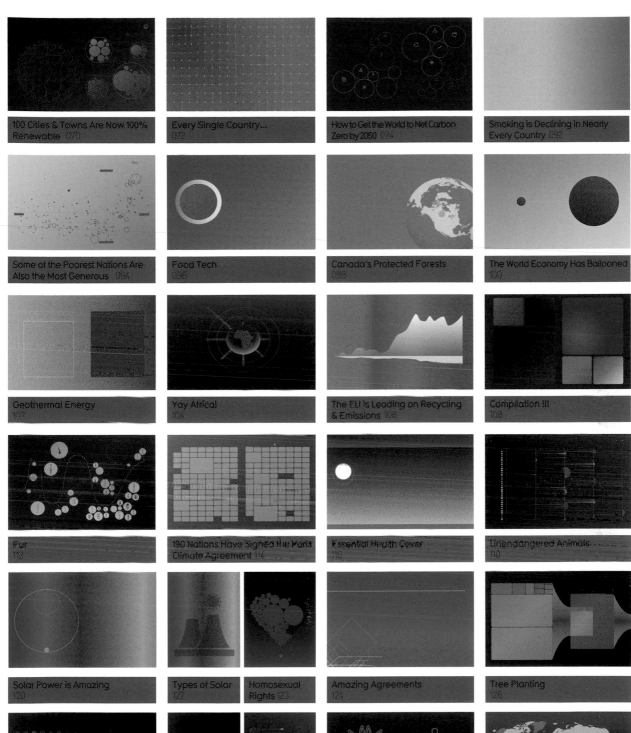

100 Cities & Towns Are Now 100% Renewable 070

Every Single Country... 072

How to Get the World to Net Carbon Zero by 2050 074

Smoking is Declining in Nearly Every Country 096

Some of the Poorest Nations Are Also the Most Generous 094

Food Tech 096

Canada's Protected Forests 098

The World Economy Has Ballooned 100

Geothermal Energy 102

Yay Africa! 104

The EU is Leading on Recycling & Emissions 106

Compilation III 108

Fur 112

190 Nations Have Signed the Paris Climate Agreement 114

Essential Health Cover 116

Unendangered Animals 118

Solar Power is Amazing 120

Types of Solar 122

Homosexual Rights 123

Amazing Agreements 124

Tree Planting 126

More Places Are Protecting Animals 130

Animals Bouncing back 132

Transport 133

Phytoplankton 134

The Kigali Amendment 136

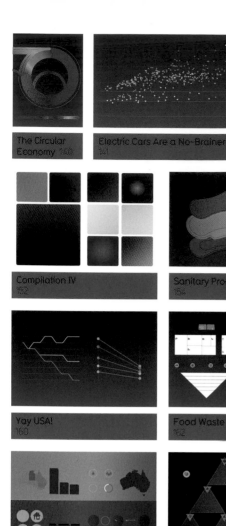
The Circular Economy 140

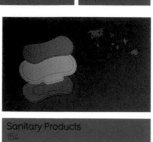
Electric Cars Are a No-Brainer 141

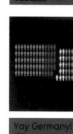
Batteries 144

Neglected Tropical Diseases 146

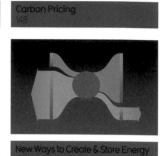
Atrica Great Wall 147

Carbon Pricing 149

Compilation IV 152

Sanitary Products 154

Yay Germany! 156

Access to Electricity 157

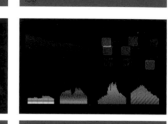
New Ways to Create & Store Energy 158

Yay USA! 160

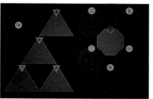
Food Waste 162

HIV/AIDS 163

Wind Power is Amazing! 164

Suicide 166

Yay Australia! 168

Magic Materials 170

A New Kind of Chocolate 172

Renewables 174

Fairphone 176

Tuberculosis 177

S. Korea's Food Waste 178

Numbers of Infections 179

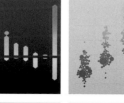
Global Tree Cover 180

Atrica Life Expectancy 181

China is... 182

Malaria 184

Plastics: The Problem 186

Types of Plastic 188

Biodegradables & Bioplastics 190

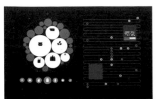

Plastic Waste & Degradation
192

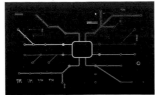

Routes for Solving Plastic
194

Creative Solutions for Plastics
196

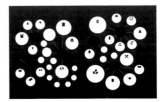

Plastics: what can you do?
198

Blood Donors
200

Death Penalty
202

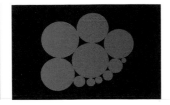

Coronavirus – Unexpected Positive
Things 204

Corporate Power Pledges
206

City & Country Climate Pledges
208

Down, down,
down 210

Land Protection
211

Surface of the
Earth 212

LEDs
213

CO2 Removal
214

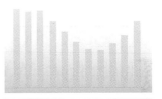

Climate Geoengineering
216

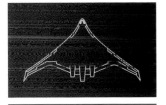

Is it Wrong to Fly?
218

Carbon Offsets
220

Fertilisers
222

De-investing from Fossil Fuels
224

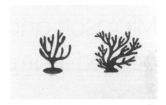

Seaweed
226

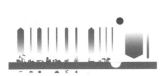

Methane
228

Hydrogen Power is Amazing!
230

Protests with more than 3.5% of
the population rarely fail 234

The Order of Things
236

Armies Around the World Are
Shrinking 238

Famine Deaths Have Plummeted
Globally 240

Everyone, Everywhere is Living Longer
242

Because Every Country is Most
Beautiful At Something 244